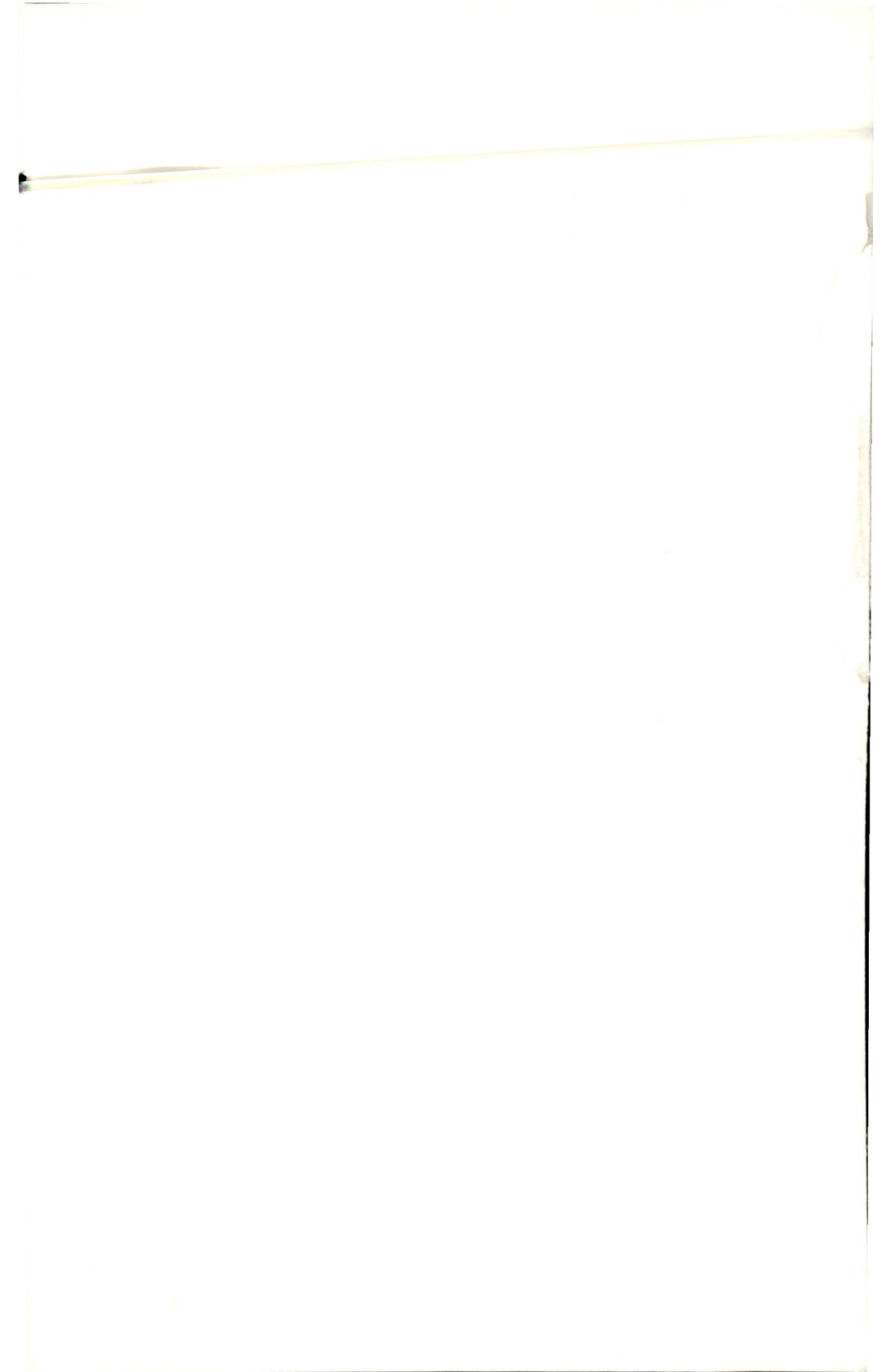

HOW TO UNLEASH YOUR AIRBNB'S FULL POTENTIAL

THE COMPLETE STEP-BY-STEP GUIDE TO MAXIMIZING BOOKINGS, RENTAL INCOME, SETTING UP AUTOMATION AND OPTIMIZATIONS FOR YOUR SHORT-TERM RENTAL BUSINESS

FRANK EBERSTADT

TABLE OF CONTENTS

INTRODUCTION

There are currently over 6 million Airbnb listings on the platform (Woodward, 2022). It is crazy to think that there are so many. This means there is a lot of competition when it comes to short-term rentals. The positive side is that business is booming, and it is a good time to be on the market. The downside is that it is very competitive, and you need to be innovative if you want to stand out from the crowd. You need to prove why your Airbnb is better than any of its competitors. This way, you can maximize your booking potential and make sure that your calendar is always full.

You may be someone who is just starting out on Airbnb, or perhaps you have been a host for quite some time. Either way, there are definitely some challenges when it comes to ensuring you meet your Airbnb's potential. Perhaps there are some seasons in the year where bookings are not as good as you would like them to be. You might've noticed a dip in your bookings, or perhaps you struggled to get your Airbnb off the ground in the first place. You may be part of a completely different group of people who have decided to increase their capacity when it comes to Airbnb and are struggling to balance everything. All of these are valid struggles. The good news is that there are solutions to all of them.

In my personal experience, all it takes is a few tools to help take your Airbnb business to the next level. I have managed to grow my short-term rental business to the point where I am making a sizable income. I started my journey small, like most of us, and by implementing the tips and tricks I will share in this book, I have increased my capacity and productivity. On top of that, I am able to deliver top-quality service to all of my guests, and I've made the entire process a lot easier for myself as well. This is what I would like to share with you—it is not something that is only possible for a few people. Every person who is in the short-term rental industry is able to maximize their growth and income.

In the world of short-term rentals, there can be a lot of confusing information. It can seem like there are always new tools and technologies that come out. This makes it difficult to decide which ones are actually going to be beneficial for you. In this book, we will go through all things Airbnb and make sure that you can choose the right avenues to increase your income and profitability. You can also make your life much easier by using technology to automate many areas of your Airbnb rental business.

This is a very exciting time in the Airbnb industry. There is a lot of growth, and if you use the right tools, you'll be able to beat the competition and make your Airbnb stand out from the rest. Eventually, you'll grow your business to the point where you have multiple vacation rentals booked out like crazy. Some strategies are incredibly simple and don't take a lot of work to implement, while others do take a bit of elbow grease to get moving. However, all of them are valuable and can add something to your Airbnb business. All you need is to know the right information so you can get moving. There has never been a better time to start, so we are going to dive right in.

UNDERSTANDING THE MARKET

Building a successful Airbnb business hinges on understanding the market. Finding out what your guests really want means you can cater to their needs and ensure they leave happy with their stay. Understanding the market allows you to predict their wants and needs, so you are always one step ahead. This leads you to outperform your competitors, setting you apart from the pack.

CONDUCTING MARKET RESEARCH

Market research is the backbone of understanding the market. It is like studying before the big exam. You need to take steps to find out the relevant information. After doing this research, you will have a much better understanding, so you can make informed decisions on your pricing, listing, and any other important aspects of running your Airbnb.

Find Out More about Your Competition

Running an Airbnb is a competitive business. Hundreds of Airbnbs near yours could offer similar benefits to guests. This means you are competing for the same pool of potential guests. Knowing as much as you can about the competition puts you in a better position to beat them. As they say, knowledge is power.

When you are looking for your direct competitors, those will be the ones in the area where your property is located. Look at the Airbnb platform to get an idea of the properties in your area. See what they are offering to guests and how they advertise themselves. You may notice a few commonalities between them, and this gives you an indication of the trends. The properties with the highest ratings and the most bookings will be the ones that are doing something right, so pay special attention to those Airbnbs. It is also a good idea to take note of their unique selling points and anything extra they offer guests.

To help keep track of all this information, you can create a spreadsheet. Fill in all the information so it is easy to read. You will be able to organize it so you can see your direct competition and the strategies that are bringing in the most money.

Compare the Pricing Models

Pricing is one of the most important things to consider when you run an Airbnb. Even if you have the most amazing property in the world, nobody is going to book with you if it is way overpriced. You will also end up losing out on a large amount of profit if you underprice your property. Understanding the pricing of the Airbnb competitors in the area will give you insight into what you can charge. When comparing, make sure

you are only comparing your prices to those of similar properties. It isn't going to work If you try to match prices for your
one-bedroom apartment with a four-bedroom house. Look for
direct competitors and develop your pricing model from there.

Look at the Reviews

The reviews of your competitors' Airbnbs give you a ton of
information. You will find out what guests liked and didn't
like. There is a chance that those same people would book an
Airbnb in the same area, and if you can provide something
that your competitors could not, you can attract new guests.
For example, you might notice a few guests were upset by
the lack of clean towels and sheets in one of your competi-
tor's Airbnbs. You can make sure you have enough of these
items in an easy-to-find closet. It would also be a good idea
to highlight this in your listing so guests know they will not
face this problem if they book with you.

Understand Your Guests

Knowing who your guests are goes a long way when it
comes to understanding their needs. It can be tempting to
try to cater to a wide variety of guests, but the problem with
doing this is that you risk missing the mark for *all* guests. It
is very difficult to cater to a family with small kids the same
way you would to a group of friends in their early 20s
looking for a good time. You will need to make compromises, and it is risky. Focusing on one type of guest will help

you zero in on what you should be providing them, and you will end up with happier customers.

Your property's location, size, and amenities will have an impact on the type of guests you attract. Make sure you consider all of this before you decide on your target market. Any reviews or feedback you receive needs to be looked into. Your guests are a wealth of information. Try not to get upset or defensive if you do get a negative review. Rather, look into it and let the guest know you will fix it for their next stay. This is especially important if the review is on public platforms. People will look at how you handled the feedback before booking with you. If you have addressed the concern, then this should not impact your bookings, and it will show that you are really concerned about meeting your guests' needs.

RECOGNIZING PEAK SEASONS AND EVENTS

Understanding your area's peak seasons and popular events helps you plan and set your prices accordingly. When accommodation is in demand, you have the opportunity to raise your prices since more people want to book. In slow seasons, you can reduce your prices to encourage people looking for a deal to book your Airbnb. Different areas will have different peak seasons. If you have a beach bungalow, summer is going to be when people want to book with you to enjoy the beach. A mountain cabin might have its peak season in winter because it's cozy, and the snow will be a fun experience for families.

Peak seasons can shift from time to time. This is why it is important to keep an eye out for what is happening in the travel world. After all the lockdowns from the pandemic a few years ago, there has been an uptick in shoulder-season travel (the period of time between a region's peak season and offseason). This means the traditional peak seasons have shifted slightly to include the few weeks before and after them. We don't know how long this trend is going to last, and there could be even more shifts in peak seasons in the future. It is a good idea to do your research on this each year so you are fully prepared.

An event can be anything that brings people to the area. There may be festivals, conferences, or showcases. It is important to stay connected with the community where your Airbnb is located, even if that is not where you live. Connecting with community groups in the area is a great way to know what is going on. When there is an event that will draw a crowd, you can raise the prices to match the demand and maximize profit.

At points in time when demand is low, you have to be a bit more aggressive when it comes to your marketing strategies. Making a few changes to your listing and requirements can make a huge difference. If you offer a discount, it is important to make this known. You can change the title of your listing to include the word "discount." This will make people more aware of the price drop. You can also reduce the minimum night requirement and change your cancellation policy to be more flexible. These small changes remove barriers and make it easier to draw people in when it's normally more difficult.

CONNECTION WITH LOCAL TOURISM OPERATORS AND BUSINESSES

Running an Airbnb is a great way to improve the community if you do it right. You are bringing more people into the area, which means you can bring in new business. Many small businesses miss out when it comes to tourism because visitors are not aware of them. As an Airbnb host, you have a unique opportunity to bring attention to these small businesses and create a stronger community.

When people go to a new city or area, they rely on the recommendations of their Airbnb host since they do not have any previous knowledge of the place. You can establish yourself as a trustworthy place by making good recommendations that are not as common and well-known. This will add to your guests' experience, and the small business owners will benefit as well.

A great way to do this is to incorporate some local treats and flavors into a welcome box for your guests. You can connect with local businesses and vendors to see if they would like to collaborate with you to get some exposure. This means you could get a discount on the items in your welcome box or get them completely free if the business owners agree. You may be able to access discounts for your guests. Perhaps free coffee or drinks with a meal are offered at certain restaurants. Another option is asking for "buy one, get one free" cards from business owners.

Incorporating the local vibe into your guests' packages is a great way to create an entire experience for them. This can be an optional add-on for them to purchase when they make the booking. Perhaps have an option for local fresh flowers to be added to the room or a local meal to be delivered to them on the day of arrival.

The options are truly endless when it comes to incorporating local businesses into your business. You get the added benefit of word of mouth. Anyone who shops at a local business you have partnered with will hear about you. This could drum up more bookings for you and make you more known among locals and those living in neighboring towns.

STRATEGIC PRICING 101

You have an amazing Airbnb in a wonderful location, but it isn't making as much money as you thought. Ever wonder why that is? Your pricing strategy could be the culprit. Sometimes, it's not about the physical Airbnb but about other factors, such as price. Price plays a huge role in whether people want to book with you. It also influences whether you make the most profit from your Airbnb.

THE BASICS OF DYNAMIC AND STATIC PRICING

There are two main strategies when it comes to pricing: dynamic and static pricing. When you are thinking of a pricing strategy, these are typically the two that would be suggested that you would think of. One tool that can be used is called Airbnb Smart Pricing. This tool will adjust your pricing depending on many different factors. It helps you keep your rates competitive without having to change the prices manually all the time. Your pricing will be automatically updated depending on what is going on in the market. If there is more demand in your area, the price will automatically go up, and in seasons where the demand is lower, it brings the prices down. This gives you a better opportunity to get bookings based on what people are looking for and is more of a dynamic pricing strategy.

Before going any further, let's discuss dynamic and static pricing. Dynamic pricing is when the price of an Airbnb listing changes as time goes on. Sometimes, people are willing to pay more for an Airbnb, and there are others when they will be looking for cheaper deals. Let's say you have a beach bungalow as your Airbnb. People will probably want to book with you in the summer when they can enjoy the beach and the sunshine. Your peak times will be during the summer holidays and weekends. Your off-peak times will be in the winter and during the week. Understandably, people are not as drawn to the beach in the colder months as in the summer months. You can charge more in the summer because people want to go on vacation. They are willing to pay more, and places will quickly get booked. In the winter months, people won't be as likely to book, so in order to draw them in, the price will need to be lower. Changing the prices depending on demand is a dynamic pricing strategy.

There is a lot to consider regarding a dynamic pricing strategy. There are plenty of ways to do it, and it sometimes takes trial and error to figure out what is going to work for you in your specific area and market. Another way to incorporate dynamic pricing into your pricing strategy is to look at the dates you have available. The most popular date could be booked up, and you have a bunch of random dates here and there that are not getting booked. This is pretty common, and it might be a good idea to use a dynamic pricing strategy to draw in some potential guests. If you bring the price down for those specific days, people are more likely to want to book with you. You would end up beating out the competition, who are all vying for a very small number of guests. In a competitive market like this, it is going to work in your favor if you do your best to beat the competition with your low prices. Just remember that you don't want to put it so low that you aren't making any profit at all.

If you use a dynamic pricing strategy, you may want to consider a few tools. These will help you access the data needed to make better choices. Many of the tools can also change the prices based on what is happening in the market, which makes things easier for you. There are quite a few tools on the market, and they are constantly being updated. Keeping up-to-date on the development of the tools in this space will allow you to choose the ones that will benefit you most. A few to look into are Airbnb's Smart Pricing, AirDNA's Smart Rates, Beyond, PriceLabs, and Wheelhouse.

Then, we have a static pricing strategy, which just means the price stays the same. You will decide on a price that suits you and leave it for the duration of your Airbnb business listing. It is much easier to handle static pricing since you do not have to change it all the time. However, the problem with this is that you are potentially missing out on revenue because you're not using a pricing strategy that changes with the market. Your pricing might work in the summer months, but it would be too expensive for people to pay in the winter months. You are now losing out on all potential guests in the winter, so your property stands vacant for a longer period of time than it should.

You can use static pricing to your advantage if you also consider adding discounts for longer stays. It is usually more beneficial for your property to be booked for a longer period of time. If someone is simply booking for one day, it can get in the way of other people being able to book. For example, somebody could book for one Saturday, and this means that any potential weekend holiday-goers will not be able to book your property. It gets in the way of them potentially booking a Friday to a Sunday, which would bring in more money. Encouraging longer booking stays helps you maximize your profit, even with a static strategy. For example, you could keep your booking price at a higher rate and then start offering discounts with more days booked. I would start with your high rate for a one-night stay, which will probably discourage people from booking one night. Then offer a 10 percent discount if the person books for two nights and a 15 percent discount if they book for three. Now, you have created the opportunity for potential guests to think about whether they can book for longer, which would discourage one-night stays. This leaves your property open for longer bookings and increases your overall revenue.

GENERAL PRICING GUIDE

Before you decide whether to use a dynamic or static pricing model, you can use a general pricing system to help you set your prices.

This will help you get the most out of your pricing without having to constantly change it or put in as much active work. Using a general pricing guide is a good idea to get your base pricing right so you know what to charge, even if you are looking to implement more dynamic strategies.

The first thing you will need to do is start researching your competition in the local area. Almost every area already has Airbnbs. This means there is already a general price that people are willing to pay in order to stay there. You can take a look at your competition to find out how much they are charging and what they are offering. If you charge too much, you risk your competitors getting all the guests, but if you charge too little, you end up losing money. Remember to only compare your property to ones that are similar to yours so you can understand what price you should use and what your potential guests would be willing to pay.

To discover the general pricing in your area, you will need to jump into the shoes of a potential guest. Log into the Airbnb platform as a guest and then start searching for properties in your area. Put in the filters that are applicable to your Airbnb and see what shows up. The next thing you will do is click on the price range filter, which will show you the average price for the date range you selected. This filter only gives you the average price, which means that any excessively expensive or cheap outliers will impact the price you are seeing. You need to exclude these outliers since they skew the average and don't give you an accurate view of what people are willing to pay. All you have to do is move the minimum price up and the maximum price down so that you remove all the outliers, and it should give you a better idea of the average price people are willing to pay.

Also, look at the number of available listings for the criteria and filters you have placed. This will give you a good idea of how many rentals are offering the same thing as you and how big your competition is. It is a good idea to check both types of information for every single month of the year, as they can change. You can create a spreadsheet for yourself to note the average nightly price and the number of listings for each month. You can then set different prices for each month, taking advantage of the changes in season. For example, in months when fewer listings are available, you can increase your price by 10 to 20 percent, as there is less competition in the area.

PRICING STRATEGIES FOR DIFFERENT PROPERTY TYPES

It is so important to fully understand your property type before you choose a pricing strategy. This is because the type of property will play a direct role in how much people are willing to pay to stay there. Someone who is just looking for a room with a bathroom is going to pay a lot less than somebody who is looking for a fully furnished apartment. When looking at your competition, you have to take into account the types of properties they have, as well as the amenities they offer. You will need to identify your direct competition in order to price your properties correctly.

When you create a listing on Airbnb, you'll be asked for your arrangement type, and there are four basic types to choose from. These are an entire home, a hotel room, a private room, and a shared room. An entire home would be the most expensive of the arrangements, while a shared room would be a lot cheaper. However, with a shared room, if you do have an entire property, it means that you can have multiple guests who stay in one home. This could result in you ending up with more profit due to the way you are listing your property on Airbnb. However, it is important to note that each arrangement type targets a specific type of guest. That is why it is important to know who your guests are and what they need so you can cater to them directly.

Amenities are such an important part of creating a pricing strategy or a price base point. Some Airbnb hosts provide the bare necessities, and others go over and above to provide more amenities for the guests. A property that has amazing amenities will be able to charge more because it offers more. Some great examples of amenities that people are willing to pay more for include hot tubs, swimming pools, gaming rooms, or even fantastic views and easy access to things like the beach.

When you are trying to figure out how much you should charge for your property, you will need to use the filters so you can see the properties that offer similar amenities to yours. It is a good idea to do a deep dive into the pricing of all the properties in your area so you can get a better idea of what they offer and how you can be different. Adding an amenity that most properties do not have in your area can be a huge benefit because it makes you stand out from the rest of the properties. Not only that, but you can start charging slightly higher rates because you are adding more value to your guests.

Now that you have a solid understanding of the basics and the most fundamental aspects of Airbnb pricing, it is time for us to dive a little deeper. In the next chapter, we are going to explore more advanced pricing strategies. These are the tools the top Airbnb hosts use to optimize their income.

3

ADVANCED PRICING STRATEGIES

Not long ago, the keywords "Airbnb collapse" were trending on Twitter. It's usually not a good idea to get your information from social media, but it was interesting to see how many people jumped on the bandwagon to say that Airbnb was going down and the prices would need to start dropping. It is no secret that many Airbnb hosts feared this becoming a reality, but the truth is that much of this can be avoided by using the right pricing strategies. Like other businesses, Airbnb goes through highs and lows in terms of average revenue. Knowing how to preempt this and ensuring that your pricing strategy matches what is going on in the market will lead you to create a sustainable and long-lasting business. Not only that, but you will be able to create an Airbnb business that brings in the maximum amount of profit possible.

Before diving into the different scenarios for changing your Airbnb pricing strategy, let's talk about it as someone who is new to the Airbnb market. When you first start out on Airbnb, you are not going to have any reviews on your listing. Reviews are the lifeblood of an Airbnb. The more reviews you have, the more people trust you and the more bookings you'll get. Someone who is new to the platform will need to focus their energy on getting positive reviews before they can start to maximize their profit. In order to do this, you need to set your price quite a bit lower than your competitors. This is so you can start attracting people to your Airbnb. Since you cannot win on reviews at this point, you will have to win on price. It does mean that you will lose out on profit, but the truth is that you need to build a base before you even have a chance to make a sustainable and long-term profit.

After you have a good number of reviews, you can start to slowly increase the price of your listing. You don't want to keep the price low for too long. Otherwise, you will be missing out on potential profit. It is usually best to make it a gradual increase rather than slapping a doubled price tag on your Airbnb. Over the course of the next few months, you will slowly increase the price until you are happy with the amount that you are charging and are sure this will bring the maximum amount of profit for you. At this point, you should have a good number of reviews, which means that you have more credibility in the market.

STRATEGIES FOR WEEKDAYS AND WEEKENDS

Setting up different prices for weekends and weekdays is pretty crucial to maximizing your Airbnb profits. Most people go away on vacation on the weekend, and if your property is a vacation rental, this will be your most in-demand time. Also, people who want to stay in the Airbnb during the week usually do so for work and are not planning to relax or enjoy the accommodation. This means they are more likely to choose the cheapest option than the option that is going to offer them the most amenities.

Many Airbnbs change their price depending on the time of the week, so you can have a look at your competitors to see how they price. This will give you a good idea of what your base price should be, and then you can work from there—on weekends when there are events happening in your area, you can increase the price even more since accommodations in that area will be in demand.

STRATEGIES FOR ORPHAN DAYS

An orphan day or an orphan period is a day or a number of days that are in between bookings. If you have a minimum night's stay on your bookings, this can create an unbookable day in between. For example, someone could book from Monday to Wednesday, and another guest could book from Thursday to Sunday. This leaves Wednesday night open. If your minimum night's stay is set to two days, then nobody will be able to book out the Wednesday, and you will essentially be losing money due to this.

One of the easiest things to do for an orphan day is to reach out to either one of your guests and ask if they would be willing to book an extra night. You can offer a good discount for this night and not issue any additional fees, such as the cleaning fee. This way, it makes booking the extra night a lot more attractive, and you don't have to worry about having a random day open that is not bringing you any money. If one of the guests says no, then you can reach out to the other guest to see if they are willing to. You would be surprised at how many people are willing to extend their stay for a discount.

If neither of the guests wants to book the orphan night and your minimum night's stay is set to two nights, you will have to change it and allow a one-night stay for that date only. You may think a one-night stay is not worth it, especially if you have set a two-night minimum and are used to multi-night stays. However, you may be surprised at how much extra profit you can make by filling the gaps in your calendar.

Earlier, I mentioned how to filter search pricing on the Airbnb platform and find out what your competition is charging. You can use this method to search your area for similar listings on the date of the orphan night. When you search for the date that the orphan night occurred, you will most likely find that most of your competition is booked for this date. If that's the case and competition is low, you can increase your price for a single night, especially if it falls on a weekend. If the orphan night occurs in a slow season or in the week, many other listings will be available, and you should create a discount to attract a booking.

STRATEGIES BASED ON LEAD TIME

A booking lead time refers to the period between when the guest makes the reservation and the day they check in. For example, your guest could make a booking on November 5 and only check in on November 25. This means the booking lead time is twenty days. You can easily find out what your average booking lead time is by using Airbnb's professional tools option. While this information is definitely accurate, it would be better for you to track your bookings to find out when people are booking your Airbnb. Remember that average booking takes into consideration outliers, and it doesn't give you accurate information that you can actually work from.

The best thing you can do is create a small spreadsheet for yourself. In one column, you will put the different booking lead times in spaces of five days. Your first column will have zero to five days, your second six to ten, and so on. You will then fill in how many bookings you get within those lead times throughout the year. This way, you have an accurate idea of when people will commonly book and when they will not. This will give you better information so you can make more informed decisions about your pricing strategy.

If you notice fewer bookings as it gets closer to the day, you can start offering discounts to encourage people to book with you. The closer you get to the actual day, the more discounts you can offer until you reach the minimum booking price that you have set for yourself. However, the opposite could be true, where you get most of your bookings closer to the stay, and most of your guests do not book in advance. Having this information on hand means you are not going to panic when you are a few weeks away from a specific open date. You know that your guests typically book with shorter notice, and you can trust that information, so you don't have to bring down your prices or offer discounts, since you can still make a maximum amount of profit even with shorter booking lead times. You can adjust your prices based on the information you have gained from your booking lead time data.

Having a deep understanding of the market and your competitors will help you make better decisions when it comes to pricing. It is also important to know what is happening in your area, in terms of events and the booking patterns that your typical Airbnb guest displays. All of this allows you to have as much information as possible when it comes to setting your prices. Being able to set strategic prices can be the difference between being profitable and struggling.

4

TRANSITIONING AND DIVERSIFICATION

I t is important to be flexible when it comes to your rental property business. There can be shifts and changes in the market that will render your current strategy ineffective. When this happens, many property investors get disheartened and sell up. Rather than looking at these situations as negatives, look at them as an opportunity to shift into something different. You will be able to maximize your profits, which will lead you to becoming more successful. A little bit of flexibility can lead to a much more stable property business year-round.

SHIFTING FROM SHORT-TERM RENTALS (STR) TO MID-TERM RENTALS (MTR)

I have personally found success using this strategy. A few years ago, after a busy summer season, I noticed that my bookings started to slow down. This was common for most hosts in my area. Weekend bookings remained strong, but fewer bookings came in during the week. Ultimately, prices started to decrease as most hosts competed for the same type of guest who stayed from Friday to Sunday.

This prompted me to start renting out my properties weekly or monthly to get through the slow season. I was happy to reduce my rate to attract longer-stay bookings. The idea of having a nearly 100 percent occupancy rate with fewer turnovers sounded good. I knew that construction had begun on a new Correctional Center that, when completed, could hold 1700 inmates. This project lasted several years. The prison was located in the middle of nowhere, and the nearest town with motels, shops, and pubs was about a twenty-minute drive away—exactly where my accommodation was situated.

There were some workers who moved to the area and rented permanent, unfurnished houses, but many companies also came for shorter periods to work on the construction site. Their workers had to stay in motels, which was costly. Airbnb listings in the area were not an option, as most hosts' calendars were already booked out for future weekends, making a month-long stay impossible in those Airbnbs.

One day, I drove to the prison's construction site, and the plan was to stick business cards on all car windshields, advertising my houses as fully furnished mid-term rentals. Unfortunately, the car park was gated, and security didn't allow me onto the construction site. Determined, I spent the next six hours parked in my car outside the construction entrance, taking note of all trucks and vans that entered or exited the site. Most of these vehicles had advertisements or company logos, so I collected their names and phone numbers. I called each one and inquired if they needed furnished mid-term accommodation. And you know what? It worked!

I managed to secure a group of temporary workers from out of town. They were initially staying in a motel, paying premium rates. We agreed on a minimum stay of six weeks with one week's notice before moving out. This group ended up staying for three months. As they left, they passed my number on to the next group of workers, who also booked with me for several weeks. This cycle continued, and those six hours spent in my car at the construction site turned out to be the best time investment for finding new guests. I accommodated carpenters, concreters, painters, electricians, plumbers, and fitters, all working on the same construction site.

Opportunities to increase business for your Airbnb are everywhere if you are willing to think outside the box. I had four solid years of mid-term bookings that brought in a steady income in the slow seasons, so those six hours in my car were totally worth it. Mid-term rentals are simply rentals that are longer than traditional short-term rentals. It bridges a gap and attracts a completely different type of guest. Many hosts do not even think of this as an option, and that means you will be one of the few who use this strategy. You will probably attract more guests and don't have to worry about not making an income in the slow periods.

Filling the Calendar with Monthly Bookings

After hearing my story, you might be thinking that shifting your strategy is a great idea—or maybe you need a little more convincing. The mid- to long-term market is increasing, and there is a definite need for more of these accommodations. The way people travel and live is changing, and this means people need places to stay on a mid-term basis. There is a rise in people who travel for work, are digital nomads, and are remote workers. These people want a place to stay so they can explore the area and don't have to worry about furnishing an apartment or staying in a hotel for a long time. Renting out your Airbnb on a long-term basis is the answer to this.

There are tons of tangible benefits that you can access when you change your strategy. One of the biggest risks associated with a short-term rental is the low turnover rate. This means it may take weeks or months before you are able to get another guest into your rental. In this case, you will have lost revenue because your property is standing empty. If you know there is a slow season coming up, it is the perfect time to start thinking about a mid-term strategy. This way, you don't have to lose out on revenue. You have the freedom to change the rates as demand increases and decreases to maximize your profit. This is not something that can be done with a long-term rental. With a mid-term rental, you get the flexibility of a short-term rental and the stability of a long-term one.

Another benefit is that it is simply easier to manage. You don't need to turn over the property every weekend. Since it is a longer stay, they will likely handle everything for themselves, and you just have to be on call in case of emergencies. You also don't have to replace items that have been used up because the guest will do their own grocery and toiletry shopping. This helps you save both time and money.

You will have peace of mind knowing that your property is bringing in money, but you don't have to do as much work. When the peak seasons roll around again, you can switch your strategy back to a short-term one so you can get the best of both worlds. Overall, you will increase your profits throughout the year and meet the needs of various types of guests.

When moving into a mid- or long-term strategy, the needs of the guests do change. Many short-term guests look for novelty and something different because they are on vacation. This is why you can attract them with themes, activities, and novelty products. However, it is not the same for mid-term and long-term guests. They are after more practicality since they are going to be calling this place home for a few weeks. You can highlight your property's more practical elements when marketing it to a new group of people. For example, you don't have to mention a welcome box or additional amenities like board games and other fun items. Rather, focus on bringing attention to Wi-Fi, a desk or office space, a quiet neighborhood, storage space, and other things that would be more attractive to someone who may be working from the location or in need of some rest after a long day at work.

INCREASING OCCUPANCY

Now that you have decided mid-term rentals are the way to go for the slower seasons, it is time to think about how you are going to increase your occupancy rates. These strategies can work with either short- or mid-term rentals; you just have to target the right audience. If you remain fluid with your approach, you will have a better chance of increasing your occupancy.

Work on Your Listing

Your listing is the most important part of attracting guests to your property. It is the first impression they get, and it will help them understand if your property is a good fit or not. Bookings are won and lost with a listing. You will need to make sure it is consistently updated and that you have all the relevant details in it. Since you are renting it out using different strategies, you should highlight when mid-term rentals are available so people are prepared for this.

In the peak seasons, your rental will target vacationers. This means your strategy will be focused on making the experience unique and enjoyable. Highlighting why potential guests should book with you is essential. There is more competition when it comes to short-term rentals, so you really need to sell it. Make it engaging and draw people in.

When you switch over to long- or mid-term rentals, people look for something different. They look for convenience and comfort. They don't want an overbearing landlord checking on them all the time and usually prefer to be left to their own devices. They will be bringing their own food and personal care items, so you will not have to worry about that. Instead, highlight what makes your property comfortable and feel like home. For example, if you have an extremely comfortable couch, you can highlight this and let them know there is nothing better than sinking into your plush sofa after a long day's work. Think about what you would want in your home away from home, and that should give you a good indication of what you should be highlighting.

Offer Discounts

Everybody loves a discount. If you offer one, you will get more people interested in your property. When moving to a mid-term strategy, you can highlight the discount guests will get if they book for a longer period of time. This will reel them in. Look at other discounts you can offer at specific times of the year, or even combine experiences with your booking. If you work with local vendors, you can get discounts for your guests for meals and activities. All of this is a huge draw.

Use Social Media

Social media is a great way to market your property. Many people just focus on the Airbnb platform, but this is a mistake. Even though you are hosting your listing on the platform, you should still market using whatever is available to you.

There is a large group of people who do not use Airbnb to find their rentals. This means you are missing out on this market. Using social media allows you to connect with them and show them what you're offering. You also have the benefit of short-form marketing, where you can make a post highlighting one aspect of your property at a time. It makes it easier for people to digest.

In today's world, people always go to social media to do research. Places with a social media presence are a lot more reputable and of better quality. This is why having this aspect of your property business really does help. It does take work, and you must be consistent with your posts to ensure you are getting the most out of social media. One of the best things you can do is plan your posts for the month. That way, you have everything ready to go. You can create and save drafts and only post them when you are ready. Set a reminder on your phone to post at specific times and days so you don't forget. All you have to do is click "post," and it will go live. It makes posting on social media a lot more manageable.

You will also need to engage with people in the comments and if they send you private messages. This boosts your credibility, and communication is always key when you are working with social media. You would be surprised at how many people get their information from the comments section of a post.

Increasing Your Airbnb's Capacity

One of the reasons someone may want to book an Airbnb rather than a hotel room is because it is bigger and more flexible. One of the best things you can do to attract more guests is to increase the capacity. All you need to do for this is add more sleeping spaces. This is an easy and cheap way to get more bookings. There could be a family with small children that needs an extra space or two.

You don't need to add an extra room to your property in order to do this. It is a simple fix. Adding a sofa bed or a bunk bed does not take up any extra space, and you get more sleeping space out of the deal. You increase your guest pool and allow more people to find you. Your listing can sleep more people, so you can add this to the listing. If you had a four-sleeper, you now have a five- or six-sleeper and are appealing to more people.

ADDITIONAL REVENUE SOURCES

There is plenty you can do to increase your revenue when you are renting out your property. This is a business, so it is important to think like a business owner. This helps you get into the mindset of finding more ways to increase revenue. The more revenue you create, the more profit you have and the more you can do with it.

Send a Questionnaire upon Booking

It is a big win to find out what your guests actually want and need. If you can give them additional services, you can make them happier and earn some extra money as well. The questionnaire does not ask them about their experience but rather creates a better one for them. You will also have the option to upsell certain things to them.

Remember to be transparent with this questionnaire and put the additional prices on it. Not every guest will want the additional services, but some will. Some ideas for additional services are a full fridge stock, airport pickup and transfers, daily cleaning, and taxi or transportation services. You can also include things like asking for their favorite wine, food, or snack in their welcome box. What you offer and ask with this questionnaire will depend on your capacity.

Customized Check-In and Checkout Times

Many guests would like to check in or check out at a different time than what is regularly stated. It takes very little effort from you to offer early or late check-in or check-out. Most guests are happy to pay extra for this. It does give you less time to turn over the property to the next guest, so bear this in mind.

Tours

If you are a resident of this area and know it well, you can offer tours. Many guests love to tour the local area and learn more about it. You could also hire a tour guide or affiliate yourself with a tour company.

Events and Celebrations

There are a huge number of guests who book an Airbnb because they are celebrating something. You can offer specific services for these celebrations. Offering a custom cake for birthdays, graduations, and anniversaries is something many guests will want. Depending on the occasion, you could also offer a celebration basket that includes champagne, a special meal, snacks, flowers, and balloons. There are tons of ways to make this work. You can add the price to the list so they are aware of it. Since many guests will be looking for places to get these items for their celebrations, you would be making their lives a lot easier.

Partner with Businesses

There are probably tons of small businesses around your Airbnb. Partnering with them will help you offer your guests unique experiences, contribute to the economy of the area, and make you some extra money. Most guests will look to you for guidance on what they should do, see, and eat in the area. Offering a custom package in which you plan their trip and guide them to all the different spots in the area helps them and you. Many businesses will be happy to offer discounts to you and your guests. Just make sure to reach out to these businesses first so you can work out a deal.

By following these transition and diversification strategies, you can ensure consistent income. But do note that successful implementation relies on understanding your performance and the market, which brings us to the next topic: data analytics and metrics.

DATA ANALYTICS AND METRICS

According to *Analytics Comes of Age* (2018), 36 percent of companies indicated that data and analytics have changed the competition in their industry. Also stated was that 32 percent of companies have changed their long-term strategies based on what they have learned from data and analytics. There is so much that can be learned. It helps you improve your strategy and takes your business to the next level.

THE POWER OF DATA ANALYTICS

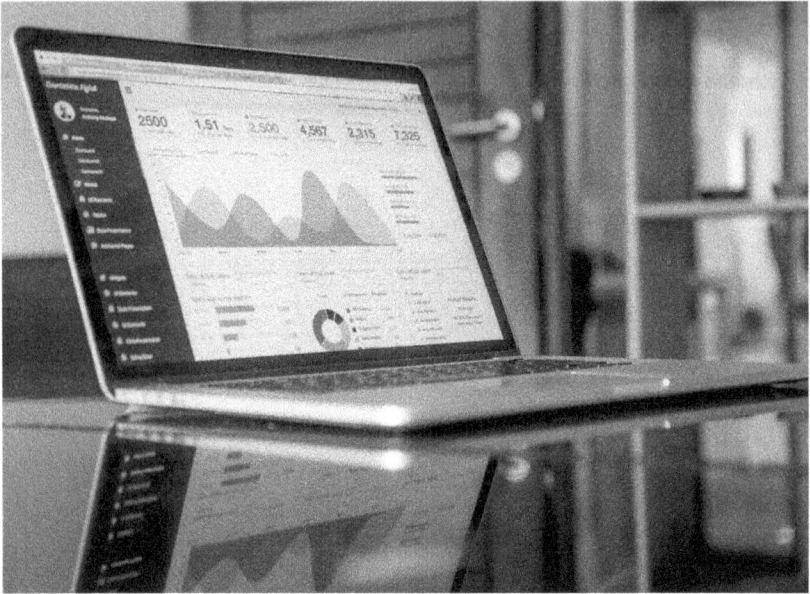

More information is always going to be better when you are making decisions and building strategies for your business. It allows you to know what is actually going on in the market so you can react appropriately. So much can change over the years that simply using the same strategy is not going to work in the long term. In this business, it is important to remain flexible throughout the process.

When you go in blind, you risk making mistakes. Using data and analytical tools means that you don't have to take that risk. You have the information in front of you, so your strategies can be based on facts and real-time data. You no longer have to use the trial-and-error approach because you can learn from what is already happening. It is like learning from other people's mistakes rather than making the same ones yourself. You know what is most effective and what is causing the most growth for others, and it will probably do the same for you.

You will find that you are far more confident with your decisions, which means you can make them a lot more quickly. When we are unsure, it takes us longer to actually get going. There is a lot of beating around the bush because we are not confident in our actions. With data, you will be more proactive and can make choices more quickly. Data will be available to you in real time so you can be more effective in your strategies and ensure they are implemented almost immediately.

Using these tools means that you can also monitor yourself and your own business. You will be able to quickly notice if there is something different with bookings or revenue. The sooner you are aware of problems, the faster you can fix them. This means you are better prepared and more aware.

There are so many tools on the market that you are spoiled for choice. You can do your own research to find one that suits you best. Just remember to look at reviews and check what they offer so you can compare them properly. Most of the good ones require you to pay a fee to use them, so you want to ensure you are paying for quality. AirDNA is one of the best tools and has been around for quite some time. It collects and provides short-term rental data for the host so they can make more informed decisions. It has access to data from over 10 million rentals, so the information you get will be well-analyzed and true. AllTheRooms and KeyData are also good options to look into.

DIFFERENT METRICS TO TRACK

Many different metrics can be tracked to help you make better decisions. A good program will have all or most of these available. Make sure to check what is offered before you buy or subscribe to data and analytics software so you can be sure you are getting what you need.

Revenue per Available Room (RevPAR)

This is an essential metric, and almost all hotels and rental properties will use it. It helps to fully understand the performance of the property at any given point. You can easily recognize any gains or losses. This metric allows you to see how well your pricing strategy is working for you. It also allows you to see your overall profitability. It is very easy to work this out. Here is the formula:

RevPAR = Average Daily Rate (ADR) × Occupancy Rate

Let's say your rental is booked 60 percent of the time, and your average daily rate is $100. This means your RevPAR is $60. You can track this to make sure you aren't dipping too low. If the overall number increases, then you know you are doing something right.

Average Daily Rate (ADR)

We used ADR to work out the previous metric, so you are probably wondering about it. This metric shows you the average amount your guests are paying per day at your rental property. Since it is common to offer discounts and there may be one-time fees applicable for a multiday booking, the nightly rate is not always accurate. Here is the formula:

$$ADR = Total\ Revenue\ /\ Number\ of\ Booked\ Nights$$

You will be using the total revenue, which means if you charge a cleaning fee or any other fee, this will need to be included. This way, you get a more accurate idea of your ADR.

Occupancy Rate

An occupancy rate can be measured using a percentage or simply by stating the number of days booked in a year. The occupancy rates are important because they affect the revenue your Airbnb makes. The more bookings a property gets, the more money it will make. Working out the occupancy rate is simple. Here is the formula:

$$Occupancy\ rate = number\ of\ booked\ nights\ /\ total\ number\ of\ nights\ available\ to\ be\ booked\ x\ 100\%$$

You will get a percentage amount, so you can see how much of your total available bookings has been taken. If it is less than 50 percent, you will need to work on increasing your bookings in some way.

Response Rate and Acceptance Rate

This is important to understand because if it is low, then you are likely not getting many bookings. Your response rate shows you how often you respond to guests within 24 hours of them reaching out. Clear communication is essential when you are running an Airbnb. Guests will be looking at multiple potential bookings; usually, the ones that respond first have a higher chance of being booked. Your acceptance rate refers to how often you accept or decline booking requests and reservations. There could be many reasons you decline a reservation, but it is not a good thing to do this for no reason. It actually reflects badly on you on the Airbnb site.

These two metrics are easily located on the platform. The acceptance rate can be found in the performance tab under "Basic Requirements." This will show you your acceptance rate for the past 365 days. Only formal booking requests count towards this, so any messages and inquiries will not count.

Cancellation and Rejection Rates

These affect how successful you are on the Airbnb platform. Airbnb only wants to suggest reliable hosts, and this means if you are rejecting and canceling too often, it will affect how often you show up in search results. If you cancel too often, your account could be suspended, which is definitely not something you want. You should not cancel more than three times a year; otherwise, suspension could be the result. You will be able to find this information under the performance tab on the platform. If guests cancel with you, then your cancellation rate will not be affected. It is best to aim for zero percent, as this means you are the most reliable.

Now that we've explored the world of data analytics and metrics, it's time to apply this knowledge to the core of your Airbnb business—your listing.

OPTIMIZING YOUR AIRBNB LISTING

A n optimized listing is your ticket to more bookings. Think about it: The first thing your guests will see is your listing. It is the first impression. In the first few seconds, your guests will decide whether your Airbnb is an option or if they should keep scrolling. You need to make your listing as appealing as possible so you can attract as many guests as possible.

WHY A COMPLETED LISTING MATTERS

Let's say you are looking to buy a house. The first place you look is on a property listing site. As you are scrolling through, you notice one that meets most of your requirements and is in your price range. Jackpot! You click on the listing, and there are only two pictures, one from the sidewalk. On top of that, the description is just one sentence. Do you bother messaging the agent? Probably not. This listing is incomplete, and that is an immediate red flag. The person who posted it clearly does not care about what they put forward, and this means that their house is not likely to be well cared for. You immediately click out and continue scrolling.

This is the same thing people do when looking at the Airbnb platform. At the end of the day, perception matters. Even if your property is the best priced and meets all its requirements, if your listing is incomplete, any potential guests will not trust you. A complete and well-done listing shows that you care about what you put out into the world, and it shows guests what they can expect. You can have all the best marketing strategies in the world, but it isn't going to matter if your listings are horrible.

The more detailed your listing, the better. Not all guests will go through every detail, but there are some who will want to. The guests who just want the basics can skim through, but at least the information is there for them should they want it. Before your guests even click on your listing, they will have a look at the cover photos. These need to draw them in, so your property's selling points need to be showcased here. Make sure all photos are of good quality. You will put the most important ones first, and then you can add all the rest after. Many guests don't read the description, but they will all look through the photos. Even if you need to hire a professional photographer, it is worth it. In my first book, *How to Set Up and Run a Successful Airbnb Business,* I go into more detail about getting the perfect pictures for your listing.

Your description is the next thing your guests might go through. It needs to be around 175 words. This is short enough not to bore them, but it also gives them enough details. Highlight key points that actually matter and that they would care about. You can also speak to the type of guest you are looking to attract. For example, if you want families to book with you, you can highlight how kid-safe and family-friendly your property is.

If you already have an Airbnb set up on the platform and have reviews, make sure you take a look at them. They might indicate things that the guests really loved and areas you can improve on. If you have taken the feedback on board and added amenities, make sure to add this to your description. These are things that your guests want, so it is important to showcase that you do have them. If your guests suggest something that would make the experience better, make sure to listen to them and do your best to get it in the future. You will be able to add the new updates to the listing. Sometimes, the smallest things make the biggest difference.

IMPROVING TITLE, DESCRIPTION, AND AMENITIES

Taking the time to craft your listing is essential. Even though they say a picture is worth a thousand words, your words also matter. Ensure you have the right title and description because this gives your potential guests the information they need. The title is what will draw them in and allow you to show up in the right search results. If the title is not appealing, you will get very few clicks. Use words that make the guest want to click rather than simply explaining the basics. Let's say you have a small property in the forest. A great title would be: Cozy Forest Hideaway. It shows the guests exactly what they can expect, but it also draws them in and allows curiosity to take over.

Your title will lead into the description, so you will need to carry the same energy over. It is so easy to just list out information, but nobody is excited to read a list. Try to tell a story with your words. This is the best way to get your point across and engage the potential guest. Your photos will give the guest a good idea of what you offer, but you need to describe the things that make your property stand out from the rest. The basics will already be listed, so you don't have to indicate the number of rooms, bathrooms, and amenities. Use this space to tell your guests about the surroundings, additional amenities, and any other unique selling points.

The additional amenities you mention should be things your guests would actually need. Knowing your guests helps you target them specifically. It is all about knowing their wants and needs before they do. If your ideal guest is someone with young kids, you must know what they would want from a vacation rental. If you have a pool or body of water close by, you could provide toys for the kids to play with, flotation devices, and canoes. If your ideal client is a businessperson, they would want an office space with quiet surroundings and good Wi-Fi. Make sure you are able to provide these things, and you will have a better chance of landing quality guests.

TIPS FOR INCREASING VISIBILITY IN SEARCH

The Airbnb platform is competitive in nature. It has been designed to help guests find the perfect place to stay. This means all the properties are fighting for attention. Making it on the platform means you need to stand out from the crowd. Your property needs to show up among the first results in the search. How many times have you scrolled to the second or third page of Google's results? Probably never. The same works for the Airbnb platform. It functions like a search engine, and you need to show up high in the search results to make an impact and get the best chance of being seen.

Airbnb SEO

SEO stands for search engine optimization. This is key when using the platform because you want to rank highly in searches. Even if you have the perfect property, it isn't going to matter unless people can actually find you. You need to know what people are searching for, and then put that in your title and description. This comes back to identifying your ideal guest and then marketing to them directly. You will still appear in search results for other people, but knowing who your target market is makes it much more effective.

A great way to find out what words you should be using is to look at the most popular properties on Airbnb that are similar to yours. Look at how they describe their properties, and look at their reviews as well. Since you are offering something very similar to them, you are going after the same guests in the area. Knowing what has made them popular will give you some ideas for doing the same.

Be Reliable

Part of Airbnb SEO is using various techniques to be more reliable and show up more in searches. The right words are important, but so are many other factors. Airbnb wants its users to make the process smooth for their guests. This is to encourage people to keep coming back to the site. If guests have a terrible time on the site, then it will affect the platform and all the hosts. That is why they focus on rewarding reliable hosts who help guests have the best experience possible.

Replying to guests and making sure you do not cancel are two ways of doing this. You will be notified when you get a message, so you will be able to answer it as soon as possible. If you don't want to be active all the time, you can set a few times in the day when you handle messages and inquiries. This way, you are still able to answer all the questions and inquiries, but you are not stuck. As long as you are responding within twenty-four hours, you should be okay, but the faster and more responsive you are, the better.

Competitive Pricing

Again, Airbnb is a competitive market. This means everyone will be pricing their Airbnbs in order to attract as many guests as possible. Believe it or not, your place on the search page is impacted by the price you charge. Airbnb will not put the most expensive properties first because this might dishearten guests looking for an affordable stay. Have a look at the prices of the Airbnbs in your area that offer the same thing, and then price from there. This way, you know you're being fair, but you're also not undercharging. Charging too little might get you a spot on the first page of the Airbnb search engine, but you are going to be losing potential revenue. It is a balancing act.

Increase Available Booking Dates

The calendar on your Airbnb page is essential. It shows when your property is available to be booked and when it is full. If you do not have the Instant Booking function enabled, then you will need to log on and refresh your calendar manually every so often so that Airbnb knows that your calendar is accurate and updated.

Instant booking makes it much easier because guests can book without your approval. It makes things a whole lot easier for everybody involved when your calendar is updated automatically. You also have a higher chance of becoming a Superhost because your response rate will go up. You will find more guests interested in your listing, and you will show up more on their radar since many guests use the Instant Book filter.

After building an irresistible and visible listing, it's time to focus on building a strong reputation that draws guests in and keeps them coming back.

BUILDING A STRONG REPUTATION

"But brand is simply a collective impression some have about a product."

— ELON MUSK

Your reputation will follow you throughout your short-term rental journey. You will get repeat guests, and people will recommend you to their friends and family. When you have met all your guests' wants and needs and they have had an amazing stay, you will be surprised at how often you get referrals from them. It is a great way to continue getting your Airbnb booked as often as possible.

BECOMING A SUPERHOST

Becoming a Superhost is one of the best things you can do for your Airbnb business. It takes a while to become a Superhost, so it's not something that you can just start off with. Knowing how to become a Superhost is essential because you can start working on it from the beginning. It requires consistent work because even once you've gotten your Superhost status, you must continue working to ensure you retain it.

Let's first start by defining what a Superhost is. A Superhost is basically like a badge or award given to a host who is recognized for having great reviews and giving excellent guest experiences. You will get an orange badge on your listing to make sure people know that you are a Superhost. There are so many benefits to becoming a Superhost. You will get increased visibility as well as more trust from your guests. There is a filter on the search engine that allows a guest to filter out anyone who is not a Superhost. If they are looking for reliable and high-quality bookings, they will do this, and you will appear in a search.

You will need to hit a few milestones in order to become a Superhost. Your response rate will need to be above 90 percent, and you will need to have hosted guests ten times in the year or have 100 nights booked with three separate reservations. Your rating must be above 4.8, and 80 percent or more of your reviews must be five stars. The final criterion is that your cancellation rate be 1 percent or lower. Airbnb will assess and grant Superhost status every few months. Be patient because even if you don't get it, you can always try again. You can check your status on the Superhost tab of the platform. It makes it easier to see how far away you are from becoming a Superhost.

COLLECTING FIVE-STAR REVIEWS

Getting those five-star reviews is essential to becoming a Superhost. The more five-star reviews you have, the better your chances are of becoming a Superhost, and you will attract more guests. Once you become a Superhost, it is easier to maintain it because you are used to putting in the effort. The first thing you need to do is make sure that your Airbnb is of good quality, comfortable, and clean. Many people get bad reviews because of the inferior cleanliness of their Airbnb. You are in direct competition with hotels, so you need to make sure that it is justified for people to book with you rather than a hotel with professional staff. You might want to hire a professional cleaner who can look over the property and clean it well. If professional cleaners are not in your budget right now, you can create a cleaning checklist for yourself to make sure that you do not miss anything.

One of the biggest mistakes that Airbnb hosts make is that they oversell their listings. If you make your property seem so amazing that meeting those standards is unrealistic, then you will not get good reviews. You need to put your best foot forward when it comes to your listing, but you also need to be honest and accurate. This way, when your guests check-in, they know what to expect, but it's also easier for you to exceed expectations and get a better review. For example, you don't have to mention there will be a welcome box or basket waiting for them. However, they will have a welcome surprise when they see this waiting for them when they check in. This enhances their experience and makes it more likely that they will give you a good review.

At the end of their stay, make sure to ask them for a review. Many guests have a great time but don't leave a review; this is a missed opportunity. Sometimes, just asking is the push they need to give you that review. If you are there when they check out, you have a better chance of connecting with them. You can ask them if they have any feedback or if there is anything negative you need to change for the next time. This way, there is a lower chance of them simply leaving a bad review if they aren't happy with something. You can reassure them that you will make the changes. You can also offer them a discount on their next stay or something similar to apologize. Explaining to them that good reviews are essential for your business means you are more likely to get their review. If they were unhappy with their stay, do not suggest they give you a review. Otherwise, it could turn out badly for you.

On the Airbnb platform, you can review your guests. This will let other Airbnb hosts know whether they should allow a booking from this type of guest. This is also a great way to prompt your guests to review you. If a guest has been a good guest, make sure you give them a positive review. For guests whose experiences were less than ideal, it's important to provide an honest and appropriate review reflecting their stay.

ENCOURAGING REPEAT GUESTS

Getting some repeat guests is really going to help with your profit, as well as make your property management easier. When you have a trusted repeat guest, you know that your property is going to be in good hands, and there will be lower marketing costs. You don't have to worry about trying to fill empty spaces because you know your guests are going to come back. This leads to a more secure and stable income, and you can build relationships and trust with your guests.

Welcome Them

First impressions really do matter a lot when you are running an Airbnb. If they have booked with you, it means that you have made a good first impression online, and now it's time to carry this through by making a good impression in person. Meeting your guests and introducing yourself is a great way to do this. It helps to establish a personal relationship with them. You can show them around and let them know that you'll be available for whatever they need. It makes many guests feel secure to know that they can put a face to the name they have been communicating with. Don't worry if you can't be available in person to meet your guest at check-in. We will cover remote check-in in the next chapter.

On the property, make sure that you have provided the basic necessities, but also try to go above and beyond. Surprising your guests with small things can really go a long way. A bottle of wine and some homemade treats can make all the difference. Also, make sure to stock things like toilet paper, fridge essentials, and other bathroom essentials so they don't have to worry about going out to find and buy these items. If they have forgotten something at home, it is already taken care of, and they can enjoy their vacation. Think about what your hotel or Airbnb offers you when you stay over. What would've made your stay smoother and more enjoyable?

Keep in Touch

Once they are ready to check out, make sure you meet them and receive the keys, so you can have a conversation with them and wish them well on their way. If you are unable to meet with your guests, don't worry too much about it now. We will cover other ways to stay in contact a bit later in the book.

This is also a great time to get any feedback and reassure them that you will be implementing it in the future. This way, it instills some excitement, so they will want to come back to see how you have improved your Airbnb.

You can also send them an email the day after they check out to thank them for staying with you. At this point, you may want to ask for a review. Once you get the review, make sure that you reply to it, whether it is positive or negative. For a positive review, you can simply thank them and let them know you are excited for the next time they stay with you. If it is a negative review, you can address the points they are concerned about and let them know that you will make the changes accordingly.

Give a Discount

Everybody loves a discount. One of the best ways to encourage people to rebook with you is to give them a discount for the next time they stay. Your discounts don't have to be for busy times. You can set these discounts or specials for times when you know bookings are typically slower. This way, you encourage people to book at those points, but you also offer them a discount, so they are incentivized to do that. They will be happy, and you will benefit from it as well.

You might even consider creating some sort of loyalty program, if it works for you. You can create an email list of all of your previous guests during the slow period. Simply send out an email with the discount exclusive to them. You would be surprised at how many people will jump at the chance to stay at an Airbnb they truly enjoy for a cheaper rate.

Your reputation is essential when it comes to building a sustainable Airbnb business. The good news is that if you do these few things, you can get there. Having established a strong reputation, let's now turn to one of the fundamental notions that underlies everything we've discussed so far: communication.

Leveling Up Airbnb Properties Across the Board

"Alone we can do so little; together we can do so much."

— HELEN KELLER

Take a moment now to think about yourself as a guest rather than an owner. If you were thorough in your research, you probably stayed in a good number of Airbnbs before you started listing yours... How many did you see had room for improvement?

Of course, every Airbnb owner wants their property to stand out from the crowd... But we also want to raise the quality of Airbnbs across the board and make our own stays (and booking experiences!) as guests more enjoyable – and this is part of my hope with this book.

So while your brain is busy thinking through all the ways you can maximize your property's potential, I'd like to ask you to take a moment to help other Airbnb owners level up their game.

That's as easy as leaving a short review – just as you want happy guests to do when they leave your property.

By leaving a review of this book on Amazon, you'll show other Airbnb owners where they can find the guidance they need to get the most out of their property – and, in

the process, you'll help raise the standard across the board.

Simply by letting other readers know how this book has helped you and what they'll find inside, you'll show them where they can find everything they need to make sure their property is fulfilling its true potential as an Airbnb destination.

Thank you so much for your support. Now, let's get back to it!

Scan the QR code below

MASTERING GUEST COMMUNICATION

One study found that 72 percent of complaints on Twitter were the result of poor customer service (Kemmis, 2022). Another 22 percent were related to scams, but we are not in the business of running scams, so this should not happen. A lot of poor customer service or unmet expectations come down to communication. If you communicate to your guests exactly what they will be receiving and everybody's on the same page, then there will be a much lower likelihood of complaints. Knowing how to properly communicate with your guests is a valuable skill when running any kind of property rental business.

AUTOMATING GUEST MESSAGES

When it comes to communication, there are a few very standard questions and concerns that are always brought up. Sometimes, this is specific to your Airbnb, and other times, it is a general question. As you spend longer in the business, you will realize what the most common queries and concerns are. This makes it a lot easier for you to develop a communication standard because you know exactly what is going to be asked.

When you are communicating with your guests, it is so important that you be transparent and available to talk to them. Many hosts want to sell their property as the best place on earth. That is understandable, but the truth is that you are setting up your guests to be disappointed. If they tell you they want a quiet location because they want to rest and relax, you might have the urge to sell your property as the perfect place for that. However, if your property is right next to a highway or close to an amusement park, you know that it's not a quiet area. While you may reassure the guests that your property is perfect for their needs, when they get there and realize there are children running around or cars driving past every five minutes, it's going to be an issue. You may get a negative review and some very unhappy guests.

Most guests are pretty forgiving when they know what to expect and when you are honest with them. Communicating well helps protect you and manage their expectations. If you have communicated something to them, then you can always go back to the conversation and show them what was agreed upon. Any important communication should always be done through email or some other kind of written medium. This way, there is a trackable history, so either of you can go back and ensure the other one is holding up their end of the bargain.

Some guests will want to communicate all the time, and others won't bother with it. Either way, it is important to make sure that the line of communication is open. There are specific moments when you should make yourself available to communicate with your guests. Firstly, it's going to be when they make an inquiry about booking with you. This is when they will have the most questions, and you should be available to answer them. Once they have booked, it is a good idea to send a message thanking them for booking with you and letting them know you are available to answer any questions or address their comments if they have any. The day before or the day of their arrival, you should send them a message to make sure they know the basics, such as the directions and check-in details, so everything goes smoothly for them. After they have checked in and are settled, you might want to check in after the first night to ask if everything has gone well and if they need anything. Once they have checked out, you can continue communication a few days after they depart to make sure they enjoyed their stay.

If you are the one who initiates most of the communication, it means that you have more control over what is going on. It is much better to be the one in control of the conversation because there is a lower likelihood of arguments and misunderstandings on your end. Sometimes, guests forget to communicate until the last minute, and then it is very difficult for you to meet their needs.

Being on point with communication can be quite difficult, especially if you are busy. This is where automated messages come in handy. You only have to create message templates, which you can copy and paste into your message field. Airbnb has a saved message feature, which makes it a lot easier. You can create as many saved messages as you would like for every occasion. You can create templates for the most commonly asked questions, booking confirmations, and welcome messages. This means that you can effectively communicate without actually having to do much.

Another option is to use a third-party site where you can completely automate the messages. This means that you don't even have to click and send the messages since it will be done on your behalf. You will have a saved message template on the software, and when specific events pop up, the right message will be sent to your guest. You could have messages for check-in and checkout, booking inquiries, booking confirmations, and cancellations. This way, the information is sent to your guests, and everybody receives the same type of communication. If there is something specific that the guest contacts you about, they can do so, as there will always be this option. Remember that even automated messages cannot cover every situation. Sometimes, speaking to your guest is going to be the best way to understand what they need or what their concerns are. Automated messages make your life a little bit easier because you don't have to continuously communicate the same thing repeatedly.

CHECK-IN OPTIONS: IN-PERSON OR REMOTE

When it comes to checking into an Airbnb, there are typically two options. The first is an in-person check-in where you, as the host, will go to meet your guests and check them in. This allows you to connect with your guests face-to-face and meet them. You will be able to show them the Airbnb and guide them through any rules or expectations, or even assist them with certain things if needed. Many hosts prefer an in-person check-in because you get to build this personal connection. They feel as though it gives them a better chance of receiving a higher review.

Remote or self-check-in options have become more popular since they are more convenient for both the host and the guest. With self-check-in, you would need to install a key lock box or smart lock on your Airbnb. A key lock box is simply a box in which you place the key that you lock using a code. You would then give the guest the code so they could access the key. With a smart lock, they would use a code to open the door of the Airbnb in order to get access. You would change the code for each new guest to enhance safety. Once the guest checks out, you can change the code so they no longer have access to the property.

This is definitely a less personal way to check in. However, there are many benefits to it. Doing an in-person check-in means that you have to be available at a certain time to check the guests in. This can be incredibly inconvenient, and if the guests are late or something unexpected happens, then you could potentially be wasting a lot of time. From the guest's perspective, it means they are limited to a specific time when they can check in and check out. Only when you are available to come and check them in and out will they be able to do so. This lack of flexibility makes the process a bit more difficult for everyone involved.

When using the self-check-in option, you need to ensure the communication is on point throughout the whole process. You will not have the opportunity to talk to your guests when they check in. This means you should send your guests a message or an email with detailed check-in instructions to smooth the process. Make sure they know what the code is and how to unlock the lock box or use the smart lock. You should still be on standby, just in case something goes wrong and they need your assistance. No technology is fully proven, so it is important to be available should something happen.

On top of all of this, you also need to make sure your guests know how to use the items in the home so they are not confused about anything. Things that you may think are common knowledge might not be for them. Since you are not there to answer their questions, having detailed instructions is really helpful. Make a book or pamphlet with instructions for the different technologies and electronics in the house. You might also want to place instruction sheets next to the relevant electronics and appliances. This does not have to be in an email since this can be in the actual home and will make it easier for them to know what instructions are for what thing.

You would also want to send them clear checkout instructions. You can do this with the check-in email you sent them, but you can also remind them when they check out. This should make things a lot smoother for them since it is easy to forget when on vacation. You will definitely have to be more intentional with your communication when you allow self-check-in, but it does make things a lot easier. You also have the opportunity to get better reviews because your guests can handle the process smoothly. As long as the communication before and during this day has been good, you don't have to worry about getting negative reviews for not being there in person for check-in. In fact, many people prefer a self-check-in, as it is a lot quicker and allows them to check in early in the morning or late in the evening if they need to.

DEALING WITH PROBLEM GUESTS

The dreaded problem guest! If you have been in the Airbnb business for a while, you have probably had a run-in with a problem guest. This is someone who is just a bad Airbnb guest and causes unnecessary issues for you. The good news is that most Airbnb guests tend to take care of the property and obey the rules. However, a small percentage of them can cause huge difficulties for you.

Learning how to deal with these guests is essential to running your Airbnb business. At the end of the day, a guest is a guest, and you want to handle the situation properly so you don't get any negative reviews. On top of that, you want to deliver excellent service as much as is within your control. This may mean you have to go a little above and beyond what you normally would to de-escalate the situation and make sure your guest is happy.

Instant Book is a great function because it allows a guest to book without you needing to confirm. It makes the whole process a lot easier, but there is a catch. When you manually confirm an Airbnb booking, you get to check their profile to see if there are any red flags. Instant Book does not allow this. If you are worried about getting a problem guest, you might consider turning off the Instant Book function and just making sure that you are on point with guest inquiries and confirming bookings. It is also important to note that reviews tend to be subjective, which means that you have to use your discretion. Sometimes, a host might give a guest a bad review that wasn't warranted in the first place. However, it is a good idea to be cautious of guests who do have negative reviews.

The next thing you need to do is make sure that your house rules are clearly laid out. Indicate that by staying at your Airbnb, they agree to the rules and terms of doing so. This means you can hold them liable for not following the rules you have established. In many cases, it is not that the guest is disrespectful, but you must remember that you could get people from various cultures, cities, and countries. The way they do things may be completely different from the way you do them. This is why you need to make sure that your expectations are clear so that everybody's on the same page. The rules that you sent out should be easy to understand and simple so there is no miscommunication. You will need to communicate this upon booking and then again when checking in. If they do not agree or don't like the rules, they simply will not stay with you, and you have avoided a bad situation.

If you encounter a situation where a guest is breaking the rules or causing a problem, you will need to deal with it directly. Many times, it could be a case of miscommunication or them simply not understanding. It is always best to communicate directly with your guests rather than getting other people involved. In many cases, you will be able to come to some agreement and move past the situation. In a dispute or disagreement, it can be easy to go on the defensive, but it's important not to blame or judge a guest. That could turn out badly for you, so handling the situation diplomatically is essential. Understand where they are coming from and what they need. It is usually best to be flexible to find a solution to the issue a guest is facing. You can offer solutions, and usually, you will come to some sort of middle ground or agreement. The main goal is to make sure your guest does not get overly emotional or upset. This could lead to irrational behavior that can be difficult to de-escalate. You need to be the calm and stable one, and if you feel that things are getting out of control, it may be best to take a step back and come back to the conversation in a few minutes. You can always talk to someone else if you need to vent, but make sure that this does not happen when you are with the guest.

If you end up in a situation where there is no middle ground and the guest is simply not listening, then you can escalate it to Airbnb. They are usually good at handling these situations. If it is a terrible situation where there may be legal issues, then you could possibly get the authorities involved. However, this is a very rare case, so you shouldn't be too concerned about that. Just remember that having the guests' best interests in mind is going to help you deal with any situation that arises in the most constructive way possible. It gives you the best chance of having a happy guest while still sticking to your standards. It might be a good option even if you have to make a few compromises until the guest leaves.

You can then never allow that guest to book with you in the future, so you will not need to deal with the situation again.

Mastering communication is just one aspect of running a successful Airbnb. It allows you to make sure that you and your guests are on the same page. This will give your guests a better experience and ensure your standards are met. But how can you manage all these tasks without consuming your entire day?

AUTOMATION AND TIME MANAGEMENT

A utomation is the future of Airbnb because it makes the entire process a lot easier for the host. When you are an Airbnb host, you will have to do quite a few things on repeat. This can get quite tedious and, frankly, annoying. Finding ways to automate these aspects makes the process easier for you so you can focus on other things. Automation is especially important for those who have multiple properties.

AUTOMATING RULESETS

When you have multiple listings on Airbnb, you can access certain Pro Tools features. This allows you to create pricing and availability rules that can be saved and applied to all or some of your listings. It makes it a lot easier to run your

Airbnb business because you don't have to keep doing the same things over and over again. Let's dive a little bit deeper into rule sets and how they work. A rule set is basically a set of parameters and rules for a specific action or thing. You will be able to name your rule set and then set the rules for how you would like things to change based on those rules.

Let's say you want to create a rule set for your nightly price. You could set a rule for adjusting the price per night based on the time of year. Your price could decrease by 10 percent during the weekdays or during low travel seasons. You may also want to create a rule set where a discount is automatically applied if the guest stays longer than a certain number of days. Other rule sets you could use are to give last-minute discounts as the day draws closer or an early bird discount if they book well in advance. You can also set things like check-in and checkout requirements, where you choose the days that a guest is able to do this. You can then apply your rule set to one or all of your listings, and it will change your current pricing and availability settings based on that.

The rules will only be applied when needed. If you have set a rule that there is a 20 percent discount on last-minute bookings, the 20 percent discount will automatically be applied to your pricing as the day draws nearer. You won't have to do anything; it will just automatically change on the Airbnb platform. When somebody books at the last minute, they will get this discounted rate. You don't have to worry about manually changing the pricing.

Using rule sets makes things so much easier. When you have multiple properties, it becomes very difficult to track exactly what is going on. You will have bookings for certain days and times based on the property, so this means there are multiple calendars to manage. You will probably be using a similar strategy across all of your properties, so using a rule set means that you don't have to be actively involved. You can develop your strategy and then just implement it across the board. You can also set rules for specific properties if you have different strategies for each one.

SCHEDULING AND AUTOMATING GUEST CHECK-INS

We touched on self-check-in in the previous chapter. This is a form of automating guest check-ins, so you don't have to be available in order for your guests to check into the Airbnb or check out when their stay is done. First, you will need to ensure you have the right equipment to automate the check-in process. This means you'll need either a smart lock, keypad, or lock box so your guests can get into the property.

The type of tool you use for self-check-in depends on your budget and what you feel is going to work best for you. Lock boxes are a pretty inexpensive way to do the self-check-in process. You'll just need to purchase a lock box and mount it on the wall near the property entrance. You will then program the lock box with a specific code that you will give to your guest on the day of check-in. They will enter the code and access the key when they arrive.

Another option is a smart lock, which is very secure and convenient. You do not need physical keys in order to use a smart lock, so it means you will have to replace the current lock with a new one. There are some smart locks that will attach to the lock that's already on the door. You will provide your guests with a passcode, and they can just enter it in order to access the house. This is actually a great option because it also eliminates the risk of the guest losing a key. These locks are great because you can integrate other software into them, such as being sent an automated message when guests check in. This message can be used to welcome guests to the property and give them relevant information about whatever is in the home.

Once you have your automated check-in set up, you just need to ensure the process is smooth for your guests. You are not going to be there to take care of them, so making sure the process is smooth is essential. You can set up a welcome box so they can easily find it as soon as they enter the Airbnb. This can be everything they need for their stay. You can have a guidebook or a house manual. This will have all the relevant information they need on this day, as well as how to use the electronics and appliances. You should also add things like the rules, Wi-Fi details, emergency contact information, and recommendations of things they can do in and around the area. This will make the guest feel a lot more at home and at ease.

Since you are not going to be there, it is important to make the welcome feel personal to them. Adding a few personal touches always goes a long way toward making them feel special and welcome. Providing a bottle of local wine or fresh flowers in the vase are nice touches that really add to the welcome experience. If the area is well known for a specific type of food or snack, then you can place these in a basket or on the counter so they can get the full experience of the area.

It is always a good idea to send your guests a checkup message at some point during their stay. This can be done in the morning after they check in because they will be settled. At this point, they might have a few questions, and you would be able to provide them with the answers. It helps them connect with you and shows you are an attentive host, even though you have not met them personally. You can automate this messaging process as well so you do not forget.

AUTOMATING OR OUTSOURCING CLEANING AND MAINTENANCE

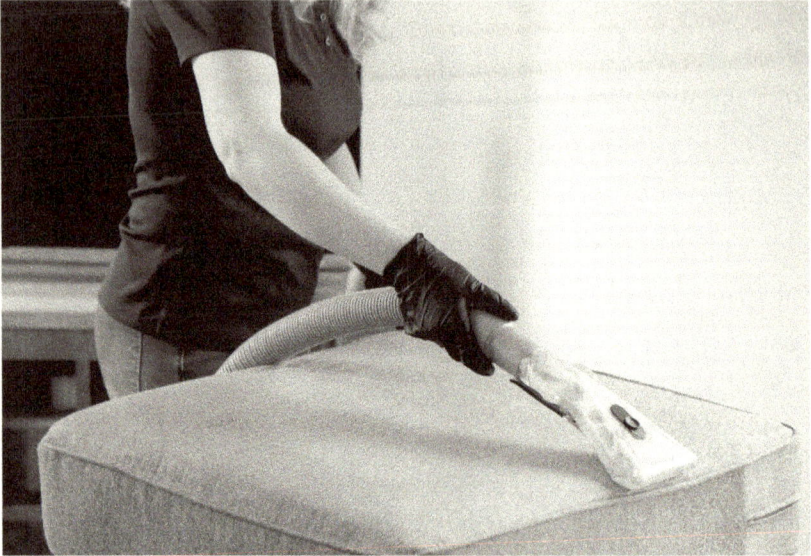

Keeping your Airbnb clean and well-maintained is crucial if you want your guests to have a good experience. If you look through reviews on Airbnb, most of the negative ones come because the house has not been well-maintained or is dirty. Cleaning and maintenance should always be at the top of your priority list, and they need to be done thoroughly so that every guest has an amazing time at your rental. If you have ever stayed at a dirty hotel, you know how uncomfortable it can be. You do not want your guests to feel the same way when they stay at your Airbnb.

As far as we have come with technology, we do not have automatic or robot cleaners just yet. Even if you do try to use some sort of robot or technology to clean, there's no guarantee that it will get everything done. You still need a human being to go in and check to make sure the property is clean and up to standard. The good news is that you have many tools at your disposal when it comes to automating your Airbnb cleaning and maintenance.

The first thing you want to do is hire a professional cleaner who will be able to get into your Airbnb and clean regularly. You can hire one from a company or go online to find one. You might even know a few professional cleaners personally, and it will make it easier to trust them if you do. It is important to get a reliable cleaner who is going to do the job well. The whole point of automating your cleaning processes is that you don't have to be involved. You want to be able to trust the cleaner, as you don't want to be called on by your guests with complaints.

If you have found a good and reliable cleaner, you will need to train them. Every Airbnb host and person has different requirements for their properties. You need to make sure that you and the cleaner are on the same page when it comes to this. One of the best ways to do this is to create a cleaning checklist. Remember that the requirements for cleaning a vacation rental are different from cleaning a regular home. When it comes to an Airbnb, it is best that the cleaner goes above and beyond to make sure that it is completely spotless. Create a checklist for each room so it's easy for the cleaner to go through it and get things done. In my previous book,

How to Set Up and Run a Successful Airbnb Business, we go through exactly how to get your Airbnb spotless and the aspects that many people overlook.

The cleaner should also be responsible for restocking the property for the next guest. This means they should have access to your inventory, so you need to have an inventory tracking process in place. This way, you know when you need to go out and buy more inventory and can make sure nothing goes missing. You can create a checklist on an app or even use a spreadsheet. You can make a list of everything that is in the inventory, as well as how many of each product there are. When the cleaner is restocking, they will simply update the spreadsheet to show the current number you have. When the numbers start getting low, then it's time for you to go shopping to replace the inventory. It is best to leave all the products in a place on the property where your guests cannot reach them, but your cleaner can easily access them. A locked cupboard or room tends to be a good option.

Now that you have all of this set up, it is important to make sure that the cleaner knows exactly when they need to go in and clean. This means they need access to your booking calendar. This way, they're able to see when people are checking out and when they're checking in. Make sure the booking calendar is as detailed as possible and includes the times your guests will be checking in and out. On the day of checkout or the day after, the cleaner will go in and clean the property as instructed. If there are any changes, you can communicate directly with the cleaner, but for the most part, the process should be completely automated.

On top of regular cleaning, you should also schedule deep-cleaning. This is especially necessary when you have many guests staying back-to-back at your property. Regular cleaning may not suffice, and there are always things that you need to get into. You can schedule this deep-cleaning when there is an empty space in the calendar. The cleaner can go in and take care of a few in-depth things related to cleaning and maintenance. This is actually incredibly valuable because it will help identify anything that needs to be replaced or maintained. Your cleaner can communicate with you if something has broken or is perishing. You will then have the information to go in and replace or fix it. These deep-cleaning sessions should happen once every few months, depending on how busy your Airbnb has been.

There is specific software that deals with this entire process to make things easier for you. It can automatically connect you with a cleaner and update your calendar on both ends so everybody knows what needs to be done. One of these apps is called "Turno," and it will handle everything for you. It is worth looking into.

Even though the entire process is going to be automated, it is still important that you be involved at some level. You will need to go in and check the property to make sure that the standards have remained the same. You don't have to do this often, especially if you trust your cleaner. However, doing spot checks every few weeks or months is always a good thing. If something needs to be changed or you want the cleaning strategy to shift a little, then you can do that or identify the problem when you are there. Overall, automating your cleaning makes everything so much easier and gives you a lot more time to focus on building a business and doing other things.

Automation and efficient time management are the backbone of a successful Airbnb business. Knowing how to do this effectively will make your life much easier. You will be saving so much time and effort. Another crucial aspect is making smart financial decisions, which we will cover in the next chapter.

FINANCIAL CONSIDERATIONS

Regardless of the type of business you have, it is very important to have a good financial strategy. This will help you take your business to the next level and ensure that your profit margins are as large as they can be. If you don't have a financial strategy, you can end up losing money in areas that you weren't even thinking of. A simple plan allows you to keep yourself organized and make sure that you are taking steps to reach a specific goal.

CHOOSING THE RIGHT CANCELLATION POLICIES

Multiple cancellation policies are available on the Airbnb platform, which is great. Choosing the right cancellation policy can have an impact on your finances. If you allow your guests to cancel up until the day they check in, this means that they do not have to pay, and it is highly unlikely that you will get somebody else to fill in that spot. This results in a loss of income. Another thing to consider is that if your cancellation policy is way too strict, people aren't going to want to book since there is no flexibility. Again, this could result in a loss of income.

Let's talk a little bit about your options when it comes to cancellation policies. Once you set up your listing on the Airbnb platform, you'll be asked to choose a cancellation policy, and there will be a brief description of what it would entail. Airbnb can change how they set up their cancellation policies, so it is always best to make sure that your information is up-to-date. However, we are going to go through the basics here so that you fully understand and can start thinking about your cancellation policy strategy.

The cancellation policies are divided into two categories. These are standard and long-term policies. You will use the standard policy when you are using your Airbnb to allow people to stay for short-term reservations. This would be less than twenty-eight consecutive nights. Long-term policies would be anything more than that, and they would override standard policy.

Underneath the category of standard policies, you have four cancellation policies. The first is a flexible cancellation policy where a guest can cancel up to twenty-four hours before the day and time of check-in. If they do that, then they will get a refund. If they cancel less than twenty-four hours before check-in, then you will be paid for the first night, but if they cancel after the check-in day, you will be paid for every night plus an additional one.

The moderate cancellation policy allows the guest to cancel up to five days before they check in. If they do this, then they will get a full refund, but if they cancel after that, you will be paid 50 percent for all nights booked that they didn't stay, plus an additional night. If they decide to stay for part of the booked nights, you'll get paid in full for each night they stay.

The firm cancellation policy entitles the guest to a full refund if they cancel more than 30 days before check-in. If they cancel between seven and thirty days before, then you will get 50 percent for all nights they have booked. If they cancel less than seven days before they are required to check in, you'll get 100 percent of the rate for every night. They are entitled to a full refund if they cancel within forty-eight hours of booking, but this only applies if they do so at least 14 days before they check in.

Next, we have a strict cancellation policy, which means that you will get 50 percent returned for all booked nights if they cancel between seven and fourteen days before they check in. If they cancel after that, you will be entitled to 100 percent of the nights. If they want a full refund, they will need to cancel within forty-eight hours of booking, which needs to be done at least fourteen days before the check-in date.

For long-term policies, you have two different cancellation policies. This is a firm, long-term cancellation policy where the guest can receive a refund if they cancel a minimum of thirty days before the check-in date. If they fail to do this, then you will get 100 percent for every night they spend at your Airbnb, plus thirty additional nights. If fewer than thirty nights remain on the reservation at the time and the guest decides to cancel, you'll get 100 percent of the remaining nights. The next policy is a strict long-term cancellation policy where the guest can be refunded if they cancel the reservation within forty-eight hours of booking, but this must be at least twenty-eight days before the date of check-in. If the guest does not abide by this, then you will get paid for every night booked, plus thirty additional nights from when they canceled. If the guest decides to cancel with less than thirty days remaining on the reservation, then you'll still get paid 100 percent for the nights remaining.

The type of cancellation policy you choose is totally up to you, but you should bear in mind that it has consequences. You will definitely attract more people with a more flexible cancellation policy. People won't feel like they are locked into something they are not sure they can commit to. Many Airbnb hosts choose a flexible cancellation policy since that generally attracts more guests. However, if you notice this does not work for you, then you can bump it up to a strict cancellation policy. This will protect your finances and make sure that you have enough time to fill the spots should someone cancel.

UNDERSTANDING THE ADDITIONAL FEES

There are multiple additional fees that can be added on when you have an Airbnb. This means there are other sources of income besides the accommodation rate you will be charging. This is a really important concept because you want to make sure you are maximizing your profit. Now, you don't want to just charge without a purpose. That can be really annoying for a guest. However, you should look at what you can charge or what additional services you can offer to your guests.

Cleaning Fees

This is a fee that you add on for the cleaning and turning over of your Airbnb. It is a one-time fee that the guest will pay. Typically, it will be included in the price the guest pays when they book. Since this is a one-time fee, it will be split over the days your guests book. So if your guests book for four nights, then the cleaning fee will be divided by four and added to each night's rate. This means that your guests will not be shocked when they go to pay and notice a fee added on.

Since the fee is added to the overall price, guests are able to filter the listing by the overall price, including fees. It gives them a more accurate idea of what they will be paying for their stay. You can charge whatever you would like as a cleaning fee. Just make sure you are not going overboard. Recently, Airbnb guests have not been happy about the cleaning fee. It is a good idea to keep an eye out on social media to see what people are saying so you know if there is a change to be made.

Some hosts prefer not to charge a cleaning fee and simply increase the nightly rate. This can work, but if you get shorter stays, you might not make enough to cover the cost of the cleaning. You also don't want to increase your nightly price so much that it becomes unreasonable for most people. A cleaning fee is just a one-time expense, so there is no danger of that.

You will need to decide how much to charge based on your property. A bigger house with multiple rooms and bathrooms should have a higher cleaning fee than a one-bedroom apartment. The average is about $50–$75, but averages can be misleading. Rather, have a look at the competition and see what they are charging. Remember to only look at properties similar to yours. This will give you an accurate idea. Another way to work out the cleaning fee is, if you use a cleaning company, to determine the company's fee. All you have to do is charge the company fee plus a little more for supplies, and that will be the cleaning fee.

Additional Guest Fees

When you set up your Airbnb listing, you get to set the initial prices and how many people it will sleep. However, you can also charge for an additional person. Sometimes, there is an unexpected guest joining them, or they have a small child who doesn't need that much space. It is important to note that your property will still have a maximum capacity and cannot accommodate more than a certain number. Sure, a person could potentially sleep on the couch, but when a guest is paying a fee, they may not be happy with that.

An extra person is an extra cost for you. Even if you don't have to add any extra furniture to accommodate them, there are utility costs, the use of toiletries, and more wear and tear. It is important to consider these things. You also don't want to charge too much for an additional person. The guest is already paying for the Airbnb. You can have a look at what your competitors are charging before you decide on your price. If you notice that the majority of your competitors are not charging this fee, it might be best to skip it. When people go to book and see a fee has been applied, they may be turned off and look for another place to stay. The fee is added to the price they see, so they should be happy with how much they are paying before they go to checkout. However, there is a breakdown of what they are paying for at the end, and this can simply turn people off when they see fees.

Pet Fees

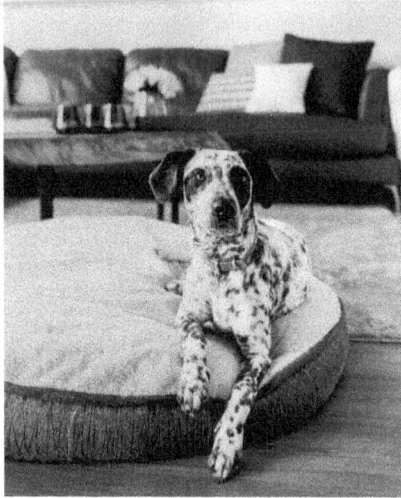

It is becoming more common for people to travel with their furry friends. This means that if you do not allow pets at all, it could end up hurting your bottom line. This is especially true if you have an outdoor type of property where dogs are able to get out and explore, or people can take them for walks. It is important to note that you will not be able to collect fees on service animals. In most cases, a service animal does not include emotional support animals, so you are able to charge for them. Make sure you check the laws in your area. For example, New York and California prohibit charging for emotional support animals.

You will be able to charge a flat fee for the pet. This will cover additional cleaning and maintenance due to having a pet in the home. You can charge per pet or have one fee for all. It is up to you. You will need to decide what fee is going to work for you, but remember to not charge too much. Around $25–$100 seems to be the average, but it depends on your property. Bigger properties can charge more since there is more to clean.

There are risks to allowing pets. Not everyone has well-trained pets. On top of that, people have different rules for their pets. If you are allowing pets in your Airbnb, then it is a good idea to have some rules and guidelines for people to follow. Mention any areas or rooms that pets would not be allowed to enter, and if you don't want pets on the furniture, make sure to mention it. With this being said, it can be difficult to enforce since you just don't know what goes on when you are not there.

By now, you've gotten a firm grasp on the financial aspects of running an Airbnb business. Yet, maximizing profits isn't just about getting your pricing and fees right; it's also about ensuring you attract enough bookings in the first place.

INNOVATIVE STRATEGIES FOR BOOSTING BOOKINGS

"Innovation distinguishes between a leader and a follower."

— STEVE JOBS

Figuring out how to boost bookings is incredibly important. It can help you increase your income, possibly even double it. The good news is that many of these strategies do not even require that much effort or more money. You will need to put in some additional work, but the profit you can get from this is definitely worth it. You don't have to do everything in this chapter.

Rather, look at what is realistic for you and what you can actually maintain. You still want to give the best service and quality to your guests.

SWITCHING TO PER-ROOM LISTING

Last-minute bookings can really help you increase your overall income. There are many people who choose to book at the last minute because of unexpected circumstances, so you can take advantage of this. In most cases, people who are booking last minute are not coming in large groups or large families. When a family or a group of people go on vacation, they typically have to plan in advance so everybody's schedule matches up. If you have a large property that can hold multiple people, you might be missing out on the last-minute booking market.

Thankfully, there is a way to still get into this market without buying an entirely new and smaller property. All you have to do is switch from renting out an entire home to a per-room listing. You have the option to divide up your property so that more people can stay at your Airbnb. If you have four bedrooms in your Airbnb, you can rent it out to four people. A single person or a couple who is looking for a last-minute booking would be happy to stay in this kind of arrangement since it would be cheaper. You would need to make your nightly rate lower than what it is for an entire property. Have a look at what people are charging in the area for one-bedroom apartments or per-room listings.

PET-FRIENDLY PROPERTIES

As mentioned in the previous chapter, there are many people who love to bring their furry friends along with them when they go on vacation. When you have an Airbnb, your main goal is to try to appeal to as large a population as possible. This will help you find a large number of guests who are willing to stay with you and pay your rates.

People who want to bring their pets are usually willing to pay a little more since fewer pet-friendly places are on the market. They are more likely to stay in an Airbnb rather than a hotel because there is more space. It is also usually cheaper to bring the pet along rather than book them into a kennel or hire someone to go to the house to feed and take care of it.

When you offer a pet-friendly listing, you'll need to make sure that the home is pet-proof. Just as people babyproof their homes, the same applies to pets. If you have any fancy little trinkets and delicate items in the home, it is best to remove them, as you don't want these things to break. You may also need to change your house rules to include pets. There might also be limitations on the type of pet that is allowed. For example, if you have a small apartment, someone would not be able to bring a large dog. You can put weight and size restrictions on the type of pet that you allow on your property. You should also stipulate that the pets who stay should be well-trained and housebroken.

This should minimize the number of accidents that happen.

It is also important that you highlight the type of pet that is allowed on your property. Even though cats and dogs are the most common pets, not everybody has them. There are some exotic pets and some that are not traditional. If you're not happy to have these in your home, then stipulate the type of pet that will be allowed. In general, if you just allow dogs, you should cover most of the people who want to bring their pets along with them.

Having a specific section for pet rules in your guest book and on your listing is a good idea. This will help the guests know exactly what is expected of them and add some security for you so you can protect your property. Things that may seem common sense to you might not be for other people, so it is important to be very specific with your rules. Highlight areas where the pets may not be permitted to enter, and state whether you allow them to be on the furniture. Make sure you have stipulated how to get rid of dog poop and cat litter. You will also need to indicate how they should keep the property clean.

Next, you need to move on to making your rental pet-friendly. When you advertise as a pet-friendly place, you need to make sure that the pets feel just as comfortable as the people. You can provide things like food and water bowls, a dog bed, toys, and a litter box or litter pick-up bags. If there are areas that are off-limits to pets, then install some fencing or gates to cordon off these areas. Another good idea is to have removable and washable covers for the furniture. This is important because even if dogs and cats are not allowed on the furniture, there is no guarantee they won't be. On top of that, they could easily rub against the furniture and cause stains and smells to stick. If the next person to check in has allergies or dislikes animals, they might be offended and unhappy with dog hair on the furniture. Easily removable and washable covers mean that you can keep things clean. Remember, you are trying to include a lot of different guests and not isolate yourself to just a pet-friendly Airbnb.

Another thing you can do is charge a higher security deposit and cleaning fee when people bring their pets along. The risk of breakage is a lot higher when there are pets, and most pet owners are aware of this. Charging high-security deposits means you are protected and will have the money to replace something if it breaks. If nothing happens, you can simply give back the security deposit, and nothing is lost on the guests' part. You can only charge a security deposit if connected through an API. We will talk more about this later on.

It is also really important that you get the property thoroughly cleaned after pets have been in it. Even if you only allow families with pets to stay at your Airbnb, making sure it's clean for the next person is essential. Animals can get worked up if too many scents of different dogs and cats are on the property. Invest in some good cleaning products that will help remove any odors. These can be a little bit more expensive, and that's why you charge a slightly higher cleaning fee.

RENTAL ARBITRAGE

Airbnb continues to expand. This means that more people do want to get into it. Whether you are thinking of getting into Airbnb or you already have a property, you can take part in rental arbitrage. It allows you to get into property rentals without actually owning property. It makes it a lot cheaper to get started, so you can increase your income.

The basics of rental arbitrage are to simply rent a property and then sublet it on the Airbnb platform. We all know that purchasing a property can be incredibly expensive, and it is becoming less and less realistic for people to do so. Growing your Airbnb business in this way means you can build a mechanism to increase your cash flow without actually owning your property and putting down a huge amount of money to get started.

You will essentially be using the income from your Airbnb to pay off the rent every month. If you play your cards right, you will be able to make quite a big profit from doing this. Now, you have to make sure that your landlord is happy for you to do this. Some landlords are quite strict and may not allow it. You don't want to sign a lease only to realize that you are not able to rent it out on Airbnb. Being completely transparent with your landlord is going to save you a lot of time and stress. You will also need to ensure that you have insurance and are protected for things like damages and injuries that take place on your property. This is part of the Aircover that Airbnb offers, but it is a good idea to get additional insurance to make sure you are completely covered.

If you have decided that rental arbitrage is something that you want to do, you need to start convincing your landlord to allow it. It is usually easier to find a property with a landlord that will allow subletting than to convince an existing contract to change. One thing to remember is that rental arbitrage is completely safe and legal, and if you follow the short-term rental laws in your state, county, or municipality, there is nothing for them to worry about.

Many landlords are under the false assumption that it is not allowed. If you come up with facts, then you'll have a better chance of succeeding. You should also show the landlord your strategy for how you plan to start an Airbnb. The risk is that they would want to do it themselves. That is why it is important to show why this is going to be beneficial for both of you since you will be handling all the work.

For example, you can let the landlord know that you will need to take much better care of the property than if you were living there. The goal is to make the most profit through Airbnb, which means giving your guests high-quality service. You will need to ensure that the amenities are working well and that your home is completely presentable, neat, and clean. On top of that, you can assure your landlord that they will be paid on time every month because you'll be running a lucrative business through the property. Since your income comes from renting out space, it will be easy for them to understand that you always have money to pay on time.

Your landlord may be concerned about the noise due to guests being in and out. They do not want to deal with this kind of disruption, so you need to reassure them that there will not be noise or parties happening in your Airbnb. There are ways that you can monitor this, such as by using noise tracking technology or stipulating there should be no noise past a certain time at the Airbnb. You will be able to enforce the rules with your guests to make sure they stick to them. Otherwise, there could be consequences.

You are presenting a strategy that will be a win-win for everyone involved. If they are already renting out their property on a long-term basis, they likely do not want to be as involved. Short-term rental means that you will need to be involved all the time to turn over the property and ensure the guests are happy. The landlord does not have to worry about any of this because you will be taking care of everything and making sure the property is well cared for.

While these innovative strategies can certainly boost your bookings and revenue, they can also introduce new risks to manage. In the next chapter, we will delve into risk management and policies to ensure your Airbnb business is not only profitable but also secure and sustainable in the long run.

RISK MANAGEMENT AND POLICIES

W hen you have an Airbnb, it is important to manage risk. There are many situations that can pop up that could cause you direct and financial harm. You don't want to be put in that position, as it can be demotivating. You can avoid most of it if you put the right measures in place.

SETTING HOUSE RULES AND SECURITY DEPOSITS

Let's first talk about house rules. This is mission-critical when you run an Airbnb. You want your guests to clearly understand what they are allowed and not allowed to do. What may be second nature to you might not be to others. Remember that people will be coming from all over the country and the world. There are different cultures and ways of doing things. If you leave things unexplained, there is no telling what will happen.

The type of rules you set will also determine the type of guests you attract. Every guest will be different, and it is important to consider why they are coming to stay with you. What might attract one guest to your Airbnb could repel another. It is also about respecting your guests. If your rules are too strict, then people will not want to stay with you. When someone is on vacation, they do not want to have a curfew, be unable to relax, or feel too restricted. You will need to filter your house rules so you stick to the ones that are actually important. If the list of rules is too long, they will likely not bother reading it. Then, they will not stick to the rules, which can cause problems. Your house rules should not be pages and pages long. Understand what matters and what you can just skip.

What you can do is set a few categories for your rules and then simply explain them within those categories. It will make it more manageable, and they will know the basics even if they do not read the full rules. Let's review a few categories and what can fall under each one. The first would be off-limits areas. There will be areas on your property that you might not want your guests snooping around. You would lock these, but it is also good to put a note in your rules. If the guests are bringing along pets or children, you might want to stipulate specific areas that should be restricted to them for their safety. You might also have storage areas, areas under construction, or general places you just don't want your guests in. Make a list of these areas under the heading of prohibited areas.

The next category would be smoking. It is up to you whether you allow smoking on your property. If you do allow it, it would be best to have designated smoking areas so your guests don't smoke anywhere they want to, which could ruin your furniture or worse. Remember that the smell of smoke is a turn-off for guests who do not smoke, so you do not want the smoke to stick to your furniture. Smoking areas should always be outside. Another category to consider is social events and parties. These can get out of hand very quickly and lead to injuries and damage to your property. If this is a big concern for you, then you can ban them entirely. You could also set rules and parameters if you do allow gatherings or parties.

Further categories would be extra guests and noise. An extra guest is an extra cost to you since they will be using the utilities and amenities. If extra guests are allowed, there should be an additional cost for them to stay the night. You can also set a limit on how many visitors can come by in a day. For noise, it will depend on where your Airbnb is situated. If it is in a remote area, it may be okay to be more easygoing. However, in a busy or residential area, there will be noise restrictions. You can set quiet hours if necessary and give general guidelines to keep the noise down.

The final category is trash. Every area and country has a different way of handling trash, which is why it is important to have guidelines and rules set out. There may be specific recycling rules in your area, so make sure your guests know about them and are able to follow them. You might also want to indicate that trash should not be left inside the property and should be properly disposed of in the designated trash containers.

There are plenty of other rule categories that you can highlight. It all depends on you and what you think is necessary. For example, specifying rules for appliance usage could be a good idea if you have specialized appliances that require specific handling.

You don't have to make these rules too long, as wordiness confuses people. Clear and concise instructions will serve you best.

Let's move on to security deposits. These are taken to cover any potential breakages or damages. The guest pays it to you, and you give it back to them in full if no damage has occurred. You cannot take a security deposit on the Airbnb platform without using API-connected software. This allows you to access the offline fee option on the platform. In other scenarios, you will not take a security deposit but instead request reimbursement for the damage caused by the guest. This will be done through the platform, and the guest's payment method will be charged. Then you will get the money for it.

Regarding damages and breakages, it is important to ask the guest first. Blindsiding them with a reimbursement request could end badly. You should always check the property as soon as you can after checkout. Make sure everything is there and accounted for. Having an inventory list for your property and all the rooms really helps. You will be able to keep track of all your items. You will be able to figure out if something is missing or broken quite quickly and can send in the reimbursement request. If you have taken a security deposit, you will check the room or home and then send the money back to them if there are no issues. If there was a problem, you could take the amount needed and send back the rest. It is a good idea to send the guest a message or email highlighting why you have issued the reimbursement or taken from the security deposit so that everyone is on the same page.

AIRBNB'S AIRCOVER

Insurance is an important part of every business, and even more so when you have a rental property. Accidents or issues can happen, and then you will need to foot the bill. This can be really expensive. Many businesses have gone down in situations like this. Most people simply do not have the money to cover large problems. Insurance steps in to help cover costs and protect you.

With Airbnb, every host has access to AirCover. It covers both liability and property damage and is automatically applied to every host. This means there are no extra steps involved. You can also get other types of insurance on your own, but AirCover will always apply. You will need to file a claim in order to get paid. The team at Airbnb will review this, and you will get a response in due course.

The property damage protection is called Airbnb Host Damage Protection. You get up to $3 million in protection for any damage caused by your guests, their visitors, or pets. The damages need to have taken place during the time between check-in and checkout. This protection also includes loss of income if the damage caused by the guest forces you to cancel future bookings. It is quite comprehensive, and it does get updated every so often. It is a good idea to go onto the Airbnb website and have a look at what it covers so you are fully prepared when the time comes. It is always best to submit a claim as soon as possible after the incident.

Getting additional insurance to cover the areas that AirCover does not cover might be a good idea. For example, AirCover does not cover damage caused by natural disasters. This means that if there were an earthquake and your property was damaged, you would have to pay cash for the repairs. In this case, it is best to get additional insurance so you are fully covered and don't have to worry about it.

Under AirCover, you also get Host Liability Insurance. This insurance program helps cover any legal responsibility you have as a host and also covers anyone who helps you, should there be some sort of issue on the property. This includes a guest or third-party getting hurt on your property or something of theirs being damaged or stolen during their stay. This insurance program gives you liability coverage for up to $1 million.

This type of insurance has been recently updated, and there are specific things it will cover. Just as with the previous type of insurance, it is important to have a look at the Airbnb website to see exactly what is covered and what is not. In general, any kind of bodily injury to the guest or other people on your property, or damage to their property while they are checked in at your Airbnb, will be covered. On top of that, it will cover damage that your guest has caused to a common area of a neighboring property. If damage has been caused but not by accident, this will not be covered. Any purposeful damage that is caused to your property by the guest is not covered. However, this is covered by the previous type of insurance.

When it comes to AirCover, it is important to understand exactly what is protected and covered. Many people get upset with AirCover simply because they do not understand the rules or what it will cover. In general, it works like many other types of insurance you can get from an insurance company. However, there are limits to what it does protect you from and what it doesn't. Remember that when you put in a claim for coverage, someone will go through the claim, do some research, and make sure that they reimburse you the necessary amount. This amount is decided based on many factors. This can mean that you don't get the results you want. For example, if you bought an antique lamp for $500, and the guest breaks it by accident, you may want to make a claim with AirCover. In your eyes, the lamp has appreciated in value, which means it has increased in value and is worth more now. However, the insurance team isn't going to take that into consideration. Instead, they will look at what you paid for the lamp and how long you've had it and then give you an amount based on that. You might only get $100 or $200 for the lamp. Sentimental value and potential value are not considered when it comes to almost any kind of insurance.

This is why knowing what to keep in your Airbnb and what you shouldn't is essential. Any sentimental or important items should be taken out, as you'll never receive the amount you believe is owed to you if something were to happen. At the end of the day, your guests probably don't even care about the antique lamp in the first place, so it's not going to add too much to your property. It is important to be smart with how you handle the layout of your property so that you can diminish the risk of accidents in the first place. Now that we have covered how to manage risks and safeguard your property, it's time to think bigger and go beyond the Airbnb platform.

EXPANDING YOUR REACH

Airbnb is a wonderful platform where you can get many benefits and tons of exposure. However, your rental property is a business first. Even if you want to be loyal to Airbnb, this might not be the best strategy for growing your business and seeking out more profit. Many different tools and platforms on the market could be really beneficial to you as you continue to grow. Considering these options could take your business to the next level.

LISTING ON MULTIPLE OTAS AND CREATING A DIRECT BOOKING SITE

Airbnb is definitely one of the larger property rental platforms. However, it is definitely not the only one. This means that just using Airbnb is costing you a few good opportunities. The goal is to reach as many people as possible so you can fill up your booking calendar. Many people prefer other platforms to Airbnb. They could be loyal to their preference, and the only way to hook them in is to be where they are.

OTA stands for online travel agency. Using multiple OTAs has tons of benefits. You get the chance to maximize your income and increase the number of bookings you get. This is the goal for most people in this business. While there are all these benefits that you can access when you use multiple different sites to promote your property, there can also be a few challenges. It is important to understand these challenges so you can navigate through them and make sure that you aren't caught off guard. You will need a good plan in place to manage the bookings for multiple sites and not get overbooked and confused. If you do not manage this properly, it can lead to some very unhappy guests who will not want to stay with you again. The good news is that there are many strategies and tools. You can use them to navigate these problems so you can get the most out of your property rental.

Different sites may need different strategies in order to be successful. There are very different requirements across the channels, so knowing what you need from each is important. You will need to optimize your listing. The better your listings are, the more clicks you will get in there, and more guests will want to book your rooms. If you spend time optimizing your listing, then you don't have to keep doing this. Great photos, SEO, an amazing title, and a compelling description are all going to play a huge part in making your listing look desirable and credible.

You also have to be prepared for the specific challenges that come with using each of the sites. Not all of them are going to be built as well as you would wish. You might notice there are things you like about each one, as well as things you dislike. It's never going to be perfect, and that's why it's best to learn how to navigate the issues instead of simply giving up. One thing you will have to consider is that you will be paying a commission on each of the websites you use. Placing a listing is usually free, but almost all of them will charge a commission for every booking made. The amount will vary; some can be up to about 20 percent. You will have to keep in mind the different commission fees that will be taken out of your nightly rate. Navigating this can be a bit tough, but you must understand the financial aspects of hosting on various platforms such as Airbnb, Booking.com, Expedia, and VRBO.

Once you have decided that this is the route you want to take because of all the benefits, you can start looking into getting a channel manager. This is a great tool because it allows you to easily host on multiple sites. It allows you to do everything from one dashboard, so you don't have to keep switching between sites, which would make the process more complicated than it needs to be. You will be able to publish your listings on as many OTAs as you would like. Since everything is available on one dashboard, it is easy for you to keep track of things. That means there is almost no risk of double booking across the various sites. You will have a calendar that you can see, and it updates on all the sites, so if somebody has booked through site one, the same dates will not be available on-site two. You will need to pay a fee to use this type of tool, but it is really worth it if you are trying to scale your business. With that being said, you don't have to jump in right away. It is easy to manage your listings if you are only posting on one or two rental sites, in which case you might not need a channel manager. Once you get to a point where you want to accelerate the growth of your business, you can consider signing up with a channel manager.

A Direct Booking Site

A direct booking site is something slightly different from what we have discussed already. With this, you'll create your own website so potential guests can go there to find all the information they need about your rentals. You will be able to market your property as well as accept direct bookings from your website. Instead of your guests using Airbnb or another site to book with you, they just need to go onto your website, and in a few clicks, they will be booked. This is how hotels work. With hotels, you can go to the actual hotel site and book your room from there. They have direct booking sites. If you want to see how this looks or works, you can go onto any hotel website and have a look.

There are many benefits to doing it this way, and it doesn't mean you cannot use Airbnb or other rental sites either. When you have your own website, you have full control over what you put on it. It becomes part of your brand, and your guests are able to see what you stand for and the quality of service you provide. If you have multiple properties, this is a great way to cross-market. Someone who had an amazing time staying at one location might want to book at another location as well. All they have to do is go onto the website and see all the different locations that you have properties in. They would expect the exact same type of service and quality each time they stay with you.

You can also use your website as a marketing tool because you get to use SEO, which helps people find you. You can use techniques such as creating blogs, newsletters, and social media to help build your brand through your website. You can put as much information as you want about your property and business on your website. When people search the internet, they will put in a few keywords. If you have these keywords on your website, you'll have a higher likelihood of showing up on the first or second page of the search results. This means that anyone looking for a property to stay in that is similar to yours would be able to find it easily.

Another benefit is that you do not have to worry about booking fees. With all other sites you post a listing on, you have to consider the commission you owe them. Since this is your own site, it's not a concern. All the money that is paid to you goes directly into your pocket. You can end up saving quite a bit of money this way.

You can hire somebody to create the website for you, but there are easy ways to do it using a website hosting provider. Typically, they will offer you all the support you need to easily build your website. You get to design it the way you want to, and you can get support as you need it. There are a few things that you have to ensure that you have. One of the most important things is a secure payment gateway. Whenever you purchase something online, you are usually redirected to a secure payment gateway. This ensures that both parties are protected, and that the money is transferred from one bank to another safely. It is also a good idea to make sure that your website is mobile-friendly because most people use the internet on their mobile phones. If the site is too difficult to navigate on a mobile device, they will probably click out and look for something else.

USING SOCIAL MEDIA FOR MARKETING

Social media is another powerful marketing tool at your disposal. Social media is also completely free. This means you can build your brand and market yourself without any monetary investment. With that being said, as you get more comfortable on social media, you can start looking at paid options that can boost your marketing strategy. Almost all successful businesses are on social media. That is because they all recognize how powerful a tool it is. Most people spend at least a few hours on social media every single day. Using it means that you get the attention of people you may not be able to connect with simply through a website or various property rental platforms.

There are different requirements that come with each type of social media platform. This means you'll need a different strategy for each one. On top of that, each social media platform shows a different kind of content and has different audiences. If you stick to only one type of social media, then you will only target a specific type of person. However, you want your reach to be as wide as possible. The good news is you can repurpose content and use it across multiple social media platforms. You might need to make a few tweaks here and there, but it is quite simple to post on various platforms.

When running social media pages for your business, you must ensure you have a plan. Pages that post consistently are the ones that get the most traction and attention. It also gives you a sense of credibility when you are constantly posting on social media. It can get overwhelming to post all the time, so one of the best things you can do is take some time to create lots of content. You can create posts and images and then simply save them as drafts. Then, once or twice a week, you can post on your social media channels. This should only take a few seconds, so it doesn't take much of your day. The best times to post are usually during the day on a workday. The truth is that there are far fewer people on social media on the weekend because everybody is busy doing things with their friends and family. People are more likely to be on social media during lunch hours and after work, which means your posts will get more views when you post at those times.

Facebook

Facebook is the original social media platform that people remember. Sure, there were definitely other social media platforms before Facebook, but Facebook has stood the test of time and continues to stand strong over the years. You can post your Airbnb listings on Facebook to generate more traction. You can easily connect your Facebook account to Airbnb, so it is easy to post your listings on Facebook. All you will need to do is go onto your Airbnb account and click on a feature called social accounts. Here, you can easily connect your Facebook account and be walked through all the steps to create a secure connection. You can also disconnect your account in the same manner if you find you no longer want it.

The first thing you want to do is create a business page for your Airbnb on Facebook. You can share information on your personal page, but that means the only people you'll be reaching are your direct friends and family. You want to reach a wider audience, so creating a dedicated page will help you do that. If you make a business page, you can also share that page on your personal social media if you want to. Having a social media page for your Airbnb means that you put forward a sense of professionalism to your potential guests. It is straightforward to set up a page. All you have to do is click "Create a page" and then follow the instructions.

Speaking about Facebook, I have created a Facebook group for Airbnb hosts to connect, share their experiences, and learn. There is so much to learn, and you can pick up some great tips from others. If you would like to join, here are the details:

Name: Airbnb Host Community

URL: www.facebook.com/groups/airbnbhostcommunity

QR Code:

Instagram

Instagram and Facebook are linked social media platforms. This means whatever you post on Instagram, you can also immediately post the same thing on Facebook. All you have to do is link the profiles, and you are good to go. That's a great advantage, as it requires minimal effort on your part. Instagram is a photo-based social media platform. Make sure you are taking high-quality pictures that you can post. You can then give a little description at the bottom and click "Share."

The great thing about a platform run with pictures is that there is a never-ending supply of content. You can give people a tour of your house, show your guests having a good time, and advertise other businesses in the area. The options are basically endless. With the new update to Instagram, you can also post video content in the form of reels. These get quite a lot of visibility if you can create content that people want to engage with. You can use the same content that you create on TikTok to post to your Instagram reel, so you're not doing double the work. We will talk about TikTok shortly.

LinkedIn

LinkedIn is a professional networking site that can also be used to market your Airbnb. Since LinkedIn is a more professional network, it is definitely more trusted, and you are more credible when you have a LinkedIn profile. It can also help you connect with people who are in the same industry as you. This can help you be part of a community where you can share ideas and grow your business in a completely different way. You can connect with other businesses that inspire you and that you want to follow. This helps you get other ideas so you can continue learning and becoming better in your field. While this may not be a strictly Airbnb marketing or social media platform, you can use it to grow your brand and connect with people who can help you build your business in the future.

TikTok

TikTok is one of the newer social media platforms, but it has grown so fast in its 7 years of existence that it is actually crazy.

With TikTok, you can post short-form video content. This takes a little more work than posting photos or status updates on other social media platforms. However, TikTok has the unique ability to make things go viral. If one of your posts goes viral, it means that thousands or even millions of people will see it. This is great exposure for your business. And don't worry, TikTok is not just for teenagers; there are millions of adults who are also on the platform.

When you have a vacation rental, you have access to travel content. Travel content is some of the most popular and watched content on TikTok. The younger and even the older generations love to travel and see various locations. If you are able to break into the niche market on TikTok, you will quickly gain a lot of traction and possibly go viral. It does take a bit of practice to learn what kinds of videos get the most views. However, a quick hack is to look at the songs that are the most popular on TikTok. If you use these songs and put them in the background of your TikTok posts, then you will have a higher chance of going viral and being seen. You can also post your TikTok videos on Instagram reels, which means you get more use out of them.

X (Twitter)

X, which was formerly known as Twitter, is another platform that you can use to market yourself on social media. The landscape has changed slightly since Elon Musk took over. There are a lot of changes taking place with the platform, which means that it may change the way brands use it to market themselves. With this platform, you will need to post short text content. This allows you to share information and your opinions on various aspects. You can post tips and tricks for traveling and staying at Airbnbs. This way, the content you post is valuable to a wide audience, and you have a higher chance of people connecting with it. You can also post pictures and videos onto the platform, so you're not just limited to text. However, it is a good idea to always include some sort of text, even if you post a video or pictures, since this is a text-based platform.

BECOMING A CO-HOST FOR OTHER AIRBNB OWNERS

Perhaps you are at a point in life where you cannot afford a property to post on Airbnb on your own. There is another option: You can become an Airbnb Co-Host. The owner of the Airbnb can decide what you have access to and can manage your payouts as well. Many Airbnb hosts do not have the time to do the work, which is why they would want a Co-Host to come in and handle most of the work for them. You will then get paid through the Airbnb platform because the host will decide on the payment split that works best for them. You can definitely negotiate if you need to.

It is important to remember that Co-Hosting is quite a bit of work. The reason you are becoming a Co-Host is to handle all the nitty-gritty aspects of renting an Airbnb. Each host is going to be completely different, so it is important to find out what they expect from you when you are Co-Hosting for them. If they give you full access to their Airbnb platform, it means that you will have access to the calendar, listings, messages, and transaction history. There are other options that allow you much less access. Some of you will only have access to the calendar; others will have access to the calendar and can message guests.

You will need to have a conversation with the host of the property so you understand exactly what your tasks will be. It is a good idea to create a resume for yourself so you can start applying for these jobs. Becoming a Co-Host is a great way to understand what is required to run your own Airbnb. It gets you a foot in the door so you can gain experience for when you host your very own property. You also get additional income from this job, which you can put towards saving for a property. In most cases, this can be a part-time job, depending on how many properties the owner has and how much work they want you to put in.

With all of this being said, you could also get a Co-Host on board for your Airbnb. If you find the work too much for you to handle, you can get a friend, family member, or someone else to become a Co-Host on the platform for you. It may make things a lot more manageable, and you will have a lot more free time and not have to worry about messaging guests and organizing the calendars.

We've explored some innovative ways to expand your reach and boost your income. But with increased scale comes increased complexity. In the next chapter, we'll delve into selecting the right management tools to help streamline operations, save time, and reduce stress.

CHOOSING THE RIGHT TOOLS
FOR MANAGEMENT

Many people are getting into Airbnb and vacation rentals because they are so profitable. The industry is absolutely booming. However, this means there is way more competition now than ever before. In order to set yourself apart from the rest, it is beneficial to look into technology-based tools. Most property managers tend to rely on these tools to help them become more effective in their jobs. Knowing which tools to use can simplify the process and make you much more productive. This results in more income and easier management of your property.

PMS AND PRICING MANAGERS

In a previous chapter, we mentioned channel managers. These tools help you manage your listings on various platforms from one dashboard. In this section, we will be talking about two other tools that could be incredibly useful in your Airbnb journey. The first one is Property Management Software (PMS).

Making sure your property is up to standard can be a difficult task. It is even more so when you have multiple properties to worry about. Using property management software makes things so much easier to keep track of. It also allows you to incorporate automation into your property management. You'll get to manage things like maintenance tasks, revenue, guest communication, and channels, all wrapped up in one box.

Maintenance management is one of the most important things when it comes to running your own Airbnb. This is something that many people forget to do because it's not at the top of their priority list. However, this results in a loss of income when something happens that needs to be repaired. This is not something you want to happen to you, so having a maintenance schedule is so important. When you have proper maintenance management software, you'll be reminded to do various maintenance tasks that directly impact the quality of your Airbnb. It allows you to streamline your tasks and automatically assign tasks to different people and vendors. This means you know the schedules are being kept and that your property is well cared for.

Another important feature of property management software is that you get access to accounting features. Money management is one of the most important things to consider when running your own business. You need to pay for things, as well as make sure you have a good profit margin. Doing this without proper software can be really difficult, especially when you have multiple properties and sources of income to consider. An accounting system will allow you to have everything in one place so you can easily see it and work from there. Your financial decisions will be much more balanced, and you can make sure you have enough money for important things.

This leads us to pricing managers, which are great tools when running an Airbnb or any vacation rental. This tool helps you automatically price your vacation rentals to optimize your pricing strategies. This way, you can make the most money with the least amount of effort. It will take into account various metrics as it works out the ideal pricing strategy for you. So many programs have this feature; some of the best include Beyond, Wheelhouse, and PriceLabs. These can be fully integrated into most property management software, and that's why it is important to choose a good one.

Here are some PMS to consider:

- Avantio
- Hostaway
- Hospitable
- Hosthub
- Hostfully
- iGMS
- Guesty
- Lodgify
- OwnerRez
- Uplisting
- Zeevou

It is always important to do your own research and make sure you have picked the one that's going to work best for you. If you want to read and compare reviews, you can go to www.capterra.com. You also have to consider the fees that come with using this technology and pick one that suits your current budget. You can always make changes later on when you have different needs. Plus, so many new types of technology keep coming on the market that you can consider.

INSTANT BOOK AND SMART PRICING

Instant Book and Smart Pricing are tools that are available on Airbnb. You can use them to help improve your property management and ensure you are getting the most out of the platform. Airbnb allows its hosts access to amazing tools that can really assist in their profitability. However, there are always advantages and drawbacks when it comes to this type of thing. You will need to decide for yourself whether these options are good for you, or if you need to seek out something else.

Let's start by talking about the Instant Book function. We have already mentioned this briefly in a previous chapter. With Instant Book, your guests can simply click and book without you confirming first. This is an amazing feature for last-minute bookings because it gives the guests security that they will have a place to stay when they book with you, and you don't have to worry about confirming before then. Not only that, but there is a filter guests can use to filter out properties that do not use Instant Book. This means your pool of potential guests will be smaller when you do not use this function.

As a host, you can receive same-day bookings when this feature is on. Someone can easily book a stay at your accommodation on the day they are going to arrive. You are able to specify when same-day and instant bookings are no longer available for that day. This means you can set a cutoff time, which makes it easier to manage. If you do not want to use same-day bookings, you can still use the Instant Book function; however, you will need to add an advance notice to your Airbnb listing. If you are using same-day booking, you may want to consider a self-check-in process so you do not have to be there to check your guests in. It'll make things a lot easier for you, and you'll still have flexibility.

Smart Pricing is another tool you can use to optimize your pricing strategy on the Airbnb platform. If you struggle with pricing, then this could be a useful tool. The tool evaluates relevant data from the property listings on Airbnb and then prices your property accordingly. It will automatically update the price depending on what is going on in the current rental market. This means if your area is in demand, you can increase the price to make more profit, and if there is a slow month, you can lower the price to still attract travelers who want a cheaper option.

It is important to note that Airbnb's smart pricing tends to set the price too low. This means you will end up losing income even though pricing is much easier to manage using the system. If this is your first time on the Airbnb platform and your property is new to the platform, then using this tool is great because you can attract people at a lower price. However, once you have gained some credibility on the platform, you may no longer want to use the smart pricing tool. There are a lot of gaps in this technology, so it is important to recognize that. It is definitely not one of the best pricing tools on the market. However, the better ones tend to be slightly more expensive. You will just need to weigh the pros and cons of using this technology versus another one. On top of that, you could manually do your own pricing and work on your pricing strategy. With all that being said,

Smart Pricing is a good option for those just getting started with their Airbnb. Just make sure to monitor and check so that you know when it is time to move on to something different so you can make more profit.

This brings us to the end of our journey through the intricacies of running a successful Airbnb business. However, this is just the beginning of your own journey. In the book's conclusion, we will review our journey together, summarize key takeaways, and, most importantly, talk about your next steps to make your Airbnb business not just survive but thrive.

Help Another Airbnb Owner Out

As a fellow Airbnb owner, you know how difficult it can be when you're first getting started – and this is your chance to make the road a little easier for someone else.

Simply by sharing your honest opinion of this book and a little about your own experience, you'll show new readers where they can find the guidance they're looking for to see success with their property listing.

JUST ONE CLICK!

Thank you for your support. I wish you the best of luck with your business.

Scan the QR code below

CONCLUSION

A great way to make a huge amount of money in the rental industry is by using effective strategies. There are so many tactics to increase your profitability and ensure your business is as successful as possible. Whether you have just started out on your Airbnb journey or you have been in the industry for quite a while, the tools you have learned will help you increase profitability and make sure you are as productive as possible.

Even implementing one or two of the things you have learned in this book will greatly help you increase your bookings. Can you imagine what would happen if you used them all? I'm not suggesting that you jump in and try to do too much at once. It is usually best to try one thing at a time so you can implement it properly before moving on to the next. The truth is that many of these tactics require time and money. You will need to plan in order to implement them properly. That way, you can ensure you are getting the most out of the tools and tricks you have learned.

As you turn the final page of this book, you're not just closing a chapter—you're opening the door to a new era of growth. Take the first step, the next, and the one after that. Ponder the area you want to improve upon, and then create a step-by-step plan to implement your decision. Start taking actionable steps toward your goal. At the end of the day, if you do not practice what you have learned, then it won't do anything for you. Taking the right steps will always yield the best results.

I wrote another book, *How to Set Up and Run a Successful Airbnb Business: Outearn Your Competition with Skyrocketing Rental Income and Leave Your 9 to 5 Job Even If You Are an Absolute Beginner.* I started this book with a powerful quote, and I will use this same quote to sign off this book.

"The longer you're not taking action, the more money you're losing."

— CARRIE WILKERSON

How to launch your own Airbnb empire from scratch — no property management experience required.

Data from Stratos Jet Charters show that **approximately 14,000 new hosts are joining Airbnb...** *every month.*

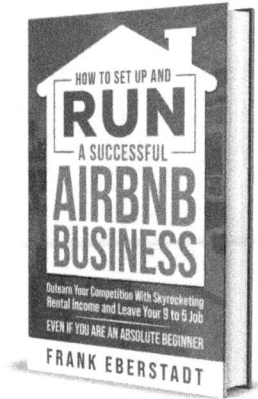

So if you plan on turning a decent profit with your Airbnb listing, you will have to find creative ways to stand out from the competition.

The good news is there's nothing to worry about.

Because the truth is anyone can start their own Airbnb rental business.

All you need are **practical strategies and principles that have been proven to work repeatedly.**

In this book, you'll discover:

- The simple **6-step framework for launching an Airbnb listing from scratch**

- The 4 primary types of Airbnb accommodations and which one you should use for your property
- How to calculate the profitability of your Airbnb listing — always look at these 5 factors
- **Airbnb Insurance: what's included and what additional coverage you might need**
- The 7 best safety tips for Airbnb hosts
- **The subtle difference between a house manual and house rules**
- **3 core components of any effective Airbnb listing** — focus on THIS element above all others
- How to automate these behind-the-scenes processes for your Airbnb business
- **9 signs that starting your own short-term rental business is the perfect fit for you**

And much more!

There's no secret "hack" to winning on Airbnb.

And unlike other guides that promote overly complex strategies filled with technical terminology… this book is designed specifically for *anyone* to understand.

So whether you're already an Airbnb host or have just discovered how Airbnb works, you'll have all the fundamental knowledge you need to start earning rental income on the side.

REFERENCES

1Angel17. (2022, November 11). *Switch to LTR?* Reddit. https://www.reddit. com/r/realestateinvesting/comments/ys49hd/switch_to_ltr

6 creative ways to collaborate with local businesses at your airbnb. (2021, August 24). Mama Mode. https://mammamode.com/6-creative-ways-to-collabo rate-with-local-businesses-at-your-airbnb/

7 steps to an unbeatable airbnb pricing strategy. (2023, February). Guest Ready. https://www.guestready.com/blog/airbnb-pricing-strategy-tips/

10 key benefits of market research. (2018, June 26). Turquoise. https://think turquoise.com/blog/market-research/10-key-benefits-of-market-research/

16 actionable ways to increase bookings during off season. (2022, August 14). Host-fully. https://www.hostfully.com/blog/more-bookings-airbnb-off-season/

70 relevant analytics statistics: 2021/2022 market share analysis & data. (2019, October 7). Finances Online. https://financesonline.com/relevant-analyt ics-statistics/

A step-by-step guide to pricing your place on airbnb. (n.d.). Padlifter. https:// padlifter.com/free-tips-and-resources/pricing/a-step-by-step-guide-to-pricing-your-place-on-airbnb/

Airbnb automated messages: A guide to guest communication. (2020, October 23). Host Tools. https://hosttools.com/blog/short-term-rental-automation/ airbnb-automated-messages/

Airbnb cleaning fee: Everything you need to know. (2023, February 2). Hospitable. https://hospitable.com/airbnb-cleaning-fees-heres-everything-you-need-to-know/

Airbnb cleaning fee: Facts and figures you should know. (2022, December 28). IGMS. https://www.igms.com/airbnb-cleaning-fee/

Airbnb co-host: Beginner's guide. (2023, May 9). Hospitable. https://hospitable. com/airbnb-co-host/

Airbnb house rules: Best examples and free template. (n.d.). Lodgify. https://www. lodgify.com/guides/airbnb-house-rules/

Airbnb instant book: Useful information for hosts. (n.d.). Lodgify. https://www.lodgify.com/guides/airbnb/instant-book/

Airbnb pricing strategies to boost your profit [master class summary]. (2020, February 3). IGMS. https://www.igms.com/airbnb-pricing/

Airbnb rental arbitrage [and how to succeed at it]. (2021, November 17). Hostfully. https://www.hostfully.com/blog/airbnb-rental-arbitrage/

Airbnb self check-in: 5 steps to automating the check-in process. (2021, February 23). Host Tools. https://hosttools.com/blog/short-term-rental-automation/airbnb-self-check-in/

Airbnb self-check-in: How it works and how to set it up. (2021, January 29). IGMS. https://www.igms.com/airbnb-self-check-in/

Airbnb smart pricing – should you use it? (2023, March 29). Floorspace. https://www.getfloorspace.com/airbnb-smart-pricing/

Airbnb tools: The complete list (2021 update). (2020, July 3). Airbnb Smart. https://airbnbsmart.com/airbnb-tools/

Amadebai, E. (2020, December 10). *13 reasons why data is important in decision making.* Analytics for Decisions. https://www.analyticsfordecisions.com/data-is-important-in-decision-making/

An in-depth guide to airbnb smart pricing [+ alternatives]. (2022, June 5). Hostfully. https://www.hostfully.com/blog/airbnb-smart-pricing-and-alternatives/

Analytics comes of age. (2018). In McKinsey Analytics. https://www.mckinsey.com/~/media/McKinsey/Business%20Functions/McKinsey%20Analytics/Our%20Insights/Analytics%20comes%20of%20age/Analytics-comes-of-age.ashx

Average airbnb prices by city [2022]. (2022). AllTheRooms. https://www.alltherooms.com/resources/articles/average-airbnb-prices-by-city/

Average daily rate (ADR) vacation rental metrics. (2018, November 26). AirDNA. https://www.airdna.co/blog/vacation-rental-metrics-adr

Average daily rate (ADR) vacation rental metrics | ADR calculation. (2018, November 26). AirDNA. https://www.airdna.co/blog/vacation-rental-metrics-adr

Booking lead time | vacation rental metrics. (2019, February 2). AirDNA - Short-Term Vacation Rental Data and Analytics. https://www.airdna.co/blog/vacation-rental-metrics-booking-lead-time

Caravitis, A. (n.d.). *How to build a direct booking website for vacation rentals for under $100.* Hosthub. https://www.hosthub.com/guides/how-to-create-your-own-direct-booking-website/

Cariaga, V. (2023, July 9). *Housing market 2023: Viral tweet says "airbnb collapse is real" — is now the time to buy a home?* Yahoo. https://finance.yahoo.com/news/housing-market-2023-viral-tweet-113009741.html?

Channel manager partners. (n.d.). Airbnb. https://www.airbnb.com/help/article/3304

Choose the right cancellation policy for you. (2020, February 5). Airbnb. https://www.airbnb.com/resources/hosting-homes/a/choose-the-right-cancellation-policy-for-you-19

Clark, R. (2021, June 28). *How to advertise your airbnb on facebook in 7 easy steps.* Lodgify. https://www.lodgify.com/blog/advertise-airbnb-facebook/

Consider your area and circumstances when pricing. (2023, May 25). Airbnb. https://www.airbnb.com/resources/hosting-homes/a/consider-your-area-and-circumstances-when-pricing-589

Dasgupta, N. (2023, July 7). *Importance of improving your quality on your airbnb listing featured.* Staah. https://blog.staah.com/featured/importance-of-improving-your-quality-on-your-airbnb-listing

Dynamic pricing strategy: Definition, types, benefits & examples. (n.d.). Paddle. https://www.paddle.com/resources/dynamic-pricing-model

Elon musk quotes. (n.d.). BrainyQuote. https://www.brainyquote.com/quotes/elon_musk_567298

Everything you need to know about the airbnb search algorithm. (n.d.). Hostaway. https://www.hostaway.com/airbnb-search-algorithm/

Freeze, P. (2022, September 20). *How to encourage repeat guests in your vacation rental.* Bay Property Management Group. https://www.baymgmtgroup.com/blog/how-to-encourage-repeat-guests-in-your-vacation-rental/

Fuchs, J. (2022, July 9). *Dynamic pricing: The complete guide.* Blog.hubspot.com. https://blog.hubspot.com/sales/dynamic-pricing#f

Hollander, J. (2023, February 16). *The 6 best airbnb pricing tools in 2023.* Hotel Tech Report. https://hoteltechreport.com/news/airbnb-pricing-tools

How do rule-sets work? (n.d.). Airbnb Help Centre. https://www.airbnb.com/help/article/2061

How does airbnb dynamic pricing drive revenue growth? (2021, May 21). IGMS. https://www.igms.com/dynamic-pricing-airbnb/

How does the airbnb cancellation policy work? (2019, March 29). Medium. https://medium.com/@airgms/how-does-the-airbnb-cancellation-policy-work-e5333b9541b2

How hosts on airbnb help support small businesses. (2020, November 25). Airbnb Newsroom. https://news.airbnb.com/how-hosts-on-airbnb-help support-small-businesses/

How smart is airbnb smart pricing and should you be using it? (2021, March 19). IGMS. https://www.igms.com/airbnb-smart-pricing/

How to automate airbnb cleaning: 6 simple tips for hosts. (n.d.). Turno. https://turno.com/automate-airbnb-cleaning/

How to charge extra fees for services: A community help guide. (2016, June 3). Airbnb Community Center. https://community.withairbnb.com/t5/Help-with-your-business/How-to-Charge-Extra-Fees-for-Services-A-Community-Help-Guide/td-p/101736

How to get good reviews on airbnb | 5-star vacation rental reviews. (n.d.). Vacasa. https://www.vacasa.com/homeowner-guides/how-to-get-good-reviews-airbnb

How to get more airbnb bookings during the off-season. (2023, January 10). Hospitable. https://hospitable.com/get-airbnb-bookings-during-off-season/

How to prepare your airbnb for peak season. (2023, May 12). AirDNA. https://www.airdna.co/blog/how-to-prepare-your-airbnb-for-peak-season

How to set a pricing strategy. (2020, December 1). Airbnb. https://www.airbnb.com/resources/hosting-homes/a/how-to-set-a-pricing-strategy-15

How to set up an effective listing page. (2020, November 18). Airbnb. https://www.airbnb.com/resources/hosting-homes/a/how-to-set-up-an-effective-listing-page-12

How to supercharge your airbnb listing with instagram. (2019, October 14). GuestReady. https://www.guestready.com/blog/airbnb-hosts-instagram/

How to switch from entire home to private room. (2018, February 12). Community.withairbnb.com. https://community.withairbnb.com/t5/Hosting/How-to-switch-from-entire-home-to-private-room/td-p/614322

How to turn your short-term rental properties into pet friendly paradises. (n.d.). Guesty. https://www.guesty.com/guide/turn-your-short-term-rental-properties-into-pet-friendly-paradises/

How to use social media to advertise airbnb property. (2021, November 24). Hosty. https://www.hostyapp.com/social-media-and-airbnb-property/

InternationalPirate. (2022, February 3). *Any positive experiences with "aircover?"*

Reddit. https://www.reddit.com/r/AirBnB/comments/sjusx2/ any_positive_experiences_with_aircover/

Is linkedin helpful for your vacation rental? (n.d.). Hostaway. https://www.host away.com/linkedin-for-your-vacation-rental/

Johnson, D. (2020, February 24). *Why and how to do market research for your vacation rental.* Simple Vacation Rental Management Software. https:// your.rentals/blog/market-research-for-your-short-term-rental-business/

Kemmis, S. (2022, May 3). *Unpopular opinion: Airbnb has become terrible.* Nerd- Wallet. https://www.nerdwallet.com/article/travel/airbnb-terrible

Krones, T. (2023). *What is an orphan period pricing rule?* Host Tools Help Center. https://help.hosttools.com/en/articles/5105363-what-is-an- orphan-period-pricing-rule

Lauzon, A. (2022, November 29). *How to research an airbnb market and quickly find a good place to buy rental property.* Mashvisor Real Estate Blog. https:// www.mashvisor.com/blog/how-to-research-airbnb-market/

Leavy, J. (2020, June 17). *How to deal with bad airbnb guests (5 tips).* AirHost Academy. https://airhostacademy.com/how-to-deal-with-bad-airbnb- guests/

McClymont, A. (2023, June 19). *Boost your airbnb success with strategic market research: Choose the perfect property to maximize....* Medium. https://medium. com/@astrid.mcclymont/how-to-choose-the-most-profitable-airbnb- property-through-market-research-b9f95a63fc61

Must-Have airbnb tools & apps. (n.d.). Hostaway. https://www.hostaway.com/ must-have-airbnb-tools-and-apps/

NoPressureLife. (2021, August 9). *All the automation ideas. give me some time back!* Reddit. https://www.reddit.com/r/airbnb_hosts/comments/ p0q9w9/all_the_automation_ideas_give_me_some_time_back/

Peña, R. (2022, June 25). *The ultimate guide: How to find rental arbitrage proper- ties.* Airbtics | Airbnb Analytics. https://airbtics.com/how-to-find-rental- arbitrage-properties/

Ribbers, J. (2019, December 10). *7 ways to boost your bottom line with airbnb add- on services.* Get Paid for Your Pad. https://getpaidforyourpad.com/blog/ additional-revenue-airbnb/

Rodriguez, A. (2022, February 20). *How to find out the airbnb demand in my area.* Mashvisor Real Estate Blog. https://www.mashvisor.com/blog/airbnb- demand-in-my-area/

Rogers, C. (2022, August 9). *Off-Season airbnb tips for higher bookings.* DPGO. https://www.dpgo.com/go/off-season-airbnb-tips-for-higher-bookings/

Scott, R. (2023, May 19). *Airbnb data and analytics to optimize your listing.* Beyond Pricing. https://www.beyondpricing.com/blog/airbnb-data-and-analytics-to-optimize-your-listing

Security deposits. (n.d.). Airbnb. https://www.airbnb.com/help/article/140

Seven ways airbnb hosts can increase revenues with a directory website. (2023, February 24). GeoDirectory. https://wpgeodirectory.com/seven-ways-airbnb-hosts-can-increase-revenues-with-a-directory-website/

Shirshikov, D. (2023, April 19). *Airbnb occupancy rate: What to expect for your property.* Awning. https://awning.com/post/airbnb-occupancy-rate

Should you list your vacation rental on multiple channels? Or stick to airbnb? (n.d.). Hostaway. https://www.hostaway.com/should-you-list-your-vacation-rental-on-multiple-channels/

Six ways that short-term vacation rentals are impacting communities. (2017, April 15). Granicus. https://granicus.com/blog/six-ways-that-short-term-vacation-rentals-are-impacting-communities/

Static vs. dynamic marketplace pricing - how to choose. (2022, July 1). StoreAutomator. https://www.storeautomator.com/blog/static-vs-dynamic-marketplace-pricing-how-to-choose/

Steve jobs quotes. (n.d.). BrainyQuote. https://www.brainyquote.com/quotes/steve_jobs_173474

Succeed at airbnb long-term rentals: Strategy and tips. (n.d.). Hostfully. https://www.hostfully.com/blog/airbnb-long-term-rentals/

Tamplin, T. (2022, May 2). *What is a financial strategy? | importance, types, and steps.* Finance Strategists. https://www.financestrategists.com/financial-advisor/financial-plan/financial-strategy/

The advantages of outsourcing airbnb cleaning to a professional service in toronto. (2023, January 25). UpMaid. https://www.upmaid.com/the-advantages-of-outsourcing-airbnb-cleaning-to-a-professional-service-in-toronto/

The basics of communicating with guests. (2020, January 8). Airbnb. https://www.airbnb.com/resources/hosting-homes/a/the-basics-of-communicating-with-guests-33

The best airbnb pricing tools in 2022 - maximize your profits with dynamic pricing. (n.d.). Floorspace. https://www.getfloorspace.com/best-airbnb-pricing-tools/

The importance of airbnb cleaning: Why a clean property is essential for providing a positive guest experience. (2023, January 3). Turnify. https://www.turnify.com/the-importance-of-airbnb-cleaning-why-a-clean-property-is-essential-for-providing-a-positive-guest-experience/

TikTok for vacation rentals: Fad or marketing opportunity? (2021, June 24). Rentals United. https://rentalsunited.com/blog/tiktok-marketing-vacation-rentals/

Top 5 property management software for airbnb [2023 guide]. (2022, September 21). Door Loop. https://www.doorloop.com/blog/property-management-software-for-airbnb

Understanding airbnb market research. (2023, June 22). IGMS. https://www.igms.com/understanding-airbnb-market-research-for-vacation-rental-hosts-a-guide-to-success/

Understanding response rate and acceptance rate. (2021, April 21). Airbnb. https://www.airbnb.com/resources/hosting-homes/a/understanding-response-rate-and-acceptance-rate-86

Understanding your market. (2023, May 25). Lloyds Bank. https://www.lloydsbank.com/business/resource-centre/business-guides/understanding-your-market.html

Using social media to market your airbnb. (n.d.). Hostaway. https://www.hostaway.com/using-social-media-to-market-your-airbnb/

van Eyk, L. (n.d.). *A landlord's guide to mid-term rentals.* Steadily. https://www.steadily.com/blog/guide-to-mid-term-rentals

Wahi, U. (2022, December 13). *How to craft authentic guest experiences by partnering with local businesses | rental scale-up.* Rental Scale Up. https://www.rentalscaleup.com/how-to-craft-authentic-guest-experiences-by-partnering-with-local-businesses/

Welcoming guests in person vs self check in - will it impact ratings? (2018, May 11). Airhostsforum. https://airhostsforum.com/t/welcoming-guests-in-person-vs-self-check-in-will-it-impact-ratings/22558

What airbnb aircover is and how it works. (n.d.). Hostaway. https://www.hostaway.com/airbnb-aircover/

What are short term rentals? (n.d.). Lodgify. https://www.lodgify.com/guides/business/short-term/

What is airbnb superhost status and is it worth getting? (2021, March 15). IGMS. https://www.igms.com/airbnb-superhost/

What is RevPAR? (2019). STR. https://str.com/data-insights-blog/what-is-revpar

What is the average airbnb pet fee? What is reasonable? (2023, April 15). BnB Facts. https://bnbfacts.com/what-is-the-average-airbnb-pet-fee-what-is-reasonable/

What to do when you receive a bad review on airbnb. (2014, March 21). Guesty. https://www.guesty.com/blog/handle-getting-bad-review/

Why you NEED airbnb dynamic pricing - expert tips. (2015, June 16). LearnBNB. https://learnbnb.com/airbnb-supply-demand-dynamic-airbnb-pricing/

Woodward, M. (2022, August 16). *Airbnb statistics [2023]: User & market growth data.* Search Logistics. https://www.searchlogistics.com/learn/statistics/airbnb-statistics/

Your airbnb pricing strategy SUCKS. (2014, August 2). LearnBNB.com. https://learnbnb.com/airbnb-pricing-strategy-sucks/

Image References

Distel, A. (2019, July 24). *Person using laptop and smartphone* [Image]. Unsplash. https://unsplash.com/photos/tLZhFRLj6nY

Dole777. (2020, January 24). *iPhone with social media icons* [Image]. Unsplash. https://unsplash.com/photos/EQSPI11rf68

Fauxels. (n.d.). *Group of Friends Making Toast* [Image]. Pexels. https://www.pexels.com/photo/group-of-friends-making-toast-3184193/

Fewings, B. (2018, August 8). *Colorful welcome sign* [Image]. Unsplash. https://unsplash.com/photos/6wAGwpsXHE0

Firmbee. (2015, May 29). *Person writing on paper* [Image]. Unsplash. https://unsplash.com/photos/gcsNOsPEXfs

Forseck, R. (2020, September 10). *Black and white dog laying on dog bed* [Image]. Unsplash. https://unsplash.com/photos/Mlrc9NwoZFk

PhotoMIX Company. (2016, Mar 17). *Documents on Wooden Surface* [Image]. Pexels. https://www.pexels.com/photo/documents-on-wooden-surface-95916/

Muza, C. (2016, April 17). *Laptop on table* [Image]. Unsplash. https://unsplash.com/photos/hpjSkU2UYSU

Trovato, G. (2023, June 8). *Woman vacuuming ottoman* [Image]. Unsplash. https://unsplash.com/photos/5TXz228u4eo

ABOUT THE AUTHOR

Frank Eberstadt is an accommodation manager and the author
of *How to Set Up and Run a
Successful Airbnb Business* & How
to Unleash Your Airbnb's Full
Potential.

His books address property
management and business
growth in Airbnb, guiding
readers to seek and capitalize on
opportunities in the market, nurturing successful businesses
on the way.

Frank is the accommodation manager for an investment
group operating hotels and motels in Australia. He has established his own successful Airbnb business, and has grown his
portfolio to six properties. Frank began his first Airbnb business from the ground up and knows how hard it can be to
break into property listings and attract guests. Using his
extensive experience in the accommodation industry, his

aim is to lay out a clear, step-by-step path that even complete newbies can follow to success.

Frank's interest in vacation property stems from his many years traveling as a solo backpacker, something he now does with his family. These two very different traveling experiences have fed into his awareness of what makes a successful vacation rental, and have been key to his success as an Airbnb business owner.

Frank still loves to travel, and enjoys surfing, but more than anything, he loves to spend quality time with his family, no matter where their adventures take them.